THE OFFICE OF A
PROPHET

THE OFFICE OF A
PROPHET

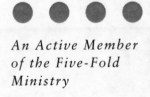

*An Active Member
of the Five-Fold
Ministry*

CHOICE NWACHUKU, Ph.D.

TATE PUBLISHING *& Enterprises*

Published by Tate Publishing & Enterprises, LLC
127 E. Trade Center Terrace | Mustang, Oklahoma 73064 USA
1.888.361.9473 | www.tatepublishing.com

Tate Publishing is committed to excellence in the publishing industry. The company reflects the philosophy established by the founders, based on Psalm 68:11,
"The Lord gave the word and great was the company of those who published it."

Book design copyright © 2011 by Tate Publishing, LLC. All rights reserved.
Cover design by Lauran Levy
Interior design by Joel Uber

Published in the United States of America

ISBN: 978-1-61739-849-0
1. Religion; Christian Ministry, General
2. Religion; Biblical Studies, Prophets
11.01.27

DEDICATION

This book is dedicated to God Almighty, who gave me the mandate and all that I needed to write in this book. I thank you, Father, for giving me grace to complete this assignment.

Table of Contents

INTRODUCTION

This book was written out of what God has been ministering to me for many years. It started from the time God called me, or should I say when I realized I was called to be a prophet (because you are called before you were born). Praise God for the family I was born into, because it is a Christian one, and from a very early age, I learned to pray and study the Word. However, I did not become born again until I was fifteen years old. From then I began to know God in a very different way, more intimately. As the relationship deepened, so did my passion for prayer and intercession. I would stay up all night praying, studying the Word, memorizing scripture, and just praising God.

Over the years, the Holy Spirit began to wake me up at night to intercede for different things. He began to show me events to pray for, people to pray for, and also different things to pray against. It became more interesting when I started seeing some of the things I was instructed to pray for happen; this made me want to pray more. Whatever church I belonged to (depending on where I was at that time), the first group I joined was always the intercessory group. This was my passion for many years and still is my passion.

As I grew as a believer, the instructions by the Holy Spirit, on specific things to pray concerning, increased. In one of my prayer sessions, I asked the LORD to add to the gift of tongues—which I already had—four specific gifts. These were prophecy, word of wisdom, word of knowledge, and discerning of spirits. I told the LORD the reason I desired and wanted these gifts was, and still is, to be more effective as an intercessor. This was my reasoning: "God, I need these gifts for people who have problems and will not share it with the church but really need someone to pray and agree with them for a breakthrough." I told God that if I was operating more in these gifts, I would know how to encourage these people more by the word of prophecy, pray for them concerning hidden problems by the word of knowledge, and advise them through the word of wisdom.

A few months after this prayer, the anointing for intercession increased with the operation in the four specific gifts I had prayed about. Then one day, some years later, my church had one of our usual all night intercessory prayer meetings, and the spirit of the LORD said to me, "Open your mouth." As I did, I felt a wave of fire enter my mouth and fill the whole of my body from my head to my feet.

The same words came to me two other times, immediately following the first word, and I experienced the same response. Then the LORD said, "I have just taken you from operating in the gifts only to the office of a prophet." And many more words accompanied this. From that day, my life changed and almost everyone I met who operated in the gift of prophecy or the office of a prophet—starting with my pastor at that time— said to me, "God has called you to be a prophet."

The Holy Spirit began to speak to me about the prophetic office, what it really entails, and how it has been misinterpreted, misunderstood, and misjudged. He also made me see that the devil was/is at work to discredit this office, hence all the controversy and persecution. The spirit of God brought to my knowledge the need for direction, instruction, and teaching for those who are called into this office so that they will not be misguided, for too many people do not understand the workings of this office. As the spirit of God revealed them to me, I asked, "But, God, do people not see these things?" His reply was, "Some do not. Some are afraid to say them for fear of persecution, and some just can't be bothered."

The spirit of God said to me, "That is why I am telling you and commissioning you not just to hear, but put it in writing for others to read and know." Then the LORD said to me, "You will not read any other material to write this book, but the Bible and I will instruct you on how it will be written. It shall be used as a study book for many in the prophetic office, and it shall set at liberty many that are bound to be released into their destinies as prophets; for it shall bring understanding and enlightenment to the body."

You see we are in a dispensation where God is releasing those in the prophetic office into the body of Christ to function, for there is an assignment to be fulfilled in this end time. I pray for all who read this book to receive understanding of the prophetic office. I specifically pray for those who will use this book as a study guide or textbook to mentor those called to the prophetic office, that the Word of God—written within its pages—will minister to your hearts and bring revelation and enlightenment. I pray that those who are called to the prophetic office will be released into their call and destiny, in the name of Jesus. I also pray that the spirit of God will give you boldness to stay in and fulfill your call, that at the end you will be able to say, like Paul, "I have kept the faith, I have fought a good fight, I have finished the work" in Jesus name, amen. God bless all who read this book.

THE FIVE-FOLD MINISTRY

The Bible clearly states that there are different areas of ministry in the body of Christ. These are apostle, prophet, evangelist, pastor, and teacher. These areas of ministry are for the effective running of the church as led by the Holy Ghost (Ephesians 4:11). There are also other gifts that are needed and in use in the body of Christ today. Of all the areas, the ministry of the apostle and prophet are less common, but now are beginning to come to the forefront.

The ministry of the prophet, or the prophetic office, is one of the most controversial of all the ministries of the church. The reason being it is the least understood. Just like all the other ministries, not everyone in the church has this calling. Ephesians 4:11 emphasizes this point by saying, "He gave some." That some, not all, are called to these different ministerial offices. This emphasis can also be read in 1 Corinthians 12:29

where it states, "Are all apostles? Are all prophets? Are all teachers?"

This gives us an understanding that not everybody will walk in the same calling.

First Corinthians 12:12-20 teaches us that the body is not one member but many and that it is God who sets the members in the body as He wants. It clearly notes the necessity of the body being diverse in ministries. This is why it reminds us that if the whole body was an ear, where would the smelling be, and if the whole body was an eye, where would the hearing be. In other words: if the church body was made up of only pastors, who would perform the work of an evangelist, of the prophet, or that of the apostle. But God saw the need for the diversities of these different callings and anointing in the body of Christ; that is why He set things in place from the beginning to be so, and we are not supposed to change it now. The Word of God is authoritative and final and should be obeyed and revered at all times.

The reason God set different ministry callings in the body was for effectiveness in the church.

> And he gave some, apostles; and some, prophets; and some, evangelists; and some, pastors and teachers; for the perfecting of the saints, for the work of the ministry, for the edifying of the body of Christ: till we all come in the unity of the faith, and of the knowledge of the Son of God, unto a perfect man, unto the measure of the stature of the fullness of Christ.
>
> Ephesians 4:11-13

God's intention for the church is that as the different areas of ministry are in operation in the church, the revelation of the Son of God, and hence God the Father, would be made known to us by the Holy Spirit. This revelation is progressive, and it is a process to be attained by the help of the Holy Ghost through the gifts Jesus has given to the church.

The goal is to become a perfect man, one who lives his life after the example of Christ. In order for this fullness to be attained in the church body, the spirit of God cannot be hindered in His operation through the different callings.

It is important that the church body recognizes that the five ministerial callings are essential to the perfecting of the saints. Therefore, it is not the person that controls the office; instead the office controls the person. That is, the office was not made for the person; the person was made for the office. A good illustration is the office of the president. The individual was not hired, and then the office created. Instead, the office was created, and then the people are hired to run the office.

The same principles apply to the ministerial callings. God, when He made the world, knew that He would have to leave it to man to govern some day. He also knew that His people would need a government to steer them in the right direction after Jesus leaves the earth. Jesus was Apostle, Prophet, Evangelist, Teacher, and Pastor to God's people while he was on the earth. Then He died, resurrected, and ascended into heaven.

After his ascension, He set in place a system through which all of these positions would continue to remain on the earth. Since the positions were created, they needed to be filled. These became the offices that make up the governing body. The purpose of this body is to direct the church by the help of the Holy Spirit on how to live to exemplify that of Christ.

The office of a prophet was the only one out of the five-fold that was very common in its function in the Old Testament. Although pastors were mentioned in the book of Jeremiah 3:15 and 10:21, they were not functioning as pastors of today because there were no churches at that time. But in the New Testament, the five-fold were all in operation. However, in the church today, the five-fold is in operation with that of the prophet being the least respected and the most persecuted. The reason for this disrespect and persecution is a result of a lack of understanding of this office, ministry rivalry on the part of some ministers occupying other offices, as well as pride and arrogance on the part of some people called into the prophetic office.

As aforementioned, every office was created for a governing purpose, which comes with responsibilities or duties. In the natural, offices carry different magnitudes of power. Good examples are the presidential office and the governor's office. It is a known fact that the presidential office has more authoritative power than the governor's office. However, the presidential office in one country holds exactly the same authoritative power to another presidential office in another country, as it relates to the citizens of each country.

As it is in the natural, so it is in the spiritual. The different ministry offices are not like the governor or the presidential offices as it compares to one another, but rather are like the president's office of each country. In other words, each office in the five-fold holds the same authoritative power toward the governing of the church body when compared to one another (Please note that I am not referring to the power made available to all Christians in the name of Jesus, which we all have, but rather about gifts that God has set in the body for effective workings in the five-fold ministry). Though they hold the same authoritative power, they differ in their job description.

This power that God has made available, known as the anointing rest, on different offices to enable individuals who work in them perform their duties or carry out their responsibilities; let us consider, for example, the presidential office. Any person who wins the election to become president takes his position in that office with all its rights and privileges. He now has more authority to make decisions concerning the country than an ordinary citizen, although he is a citizen just like the other people. The same applies to the ministerial offices. The people called to these positions are Christians like other believers with all the rights and privileges as God's children, but with specific anointings and manifestations of gifts that may be peculiar to them, because of their position as teachers, evangelists, pastors, prophets, and apostles. This peculiar anointings are given to help such a person to be effective and successful in the work that God has committed to them.

The purpose of this study is to help bring understanding and enlightenment to the office of a prophet by stressing the responsibilities and gifts the office confers on those who are called to occupy it as well as the types of prophecies delivered by them.

Responsibilities of the Prophetic Office

It is imperative that the reader understands that there are responsibilities as well as privileges (rights) accorded to those who are called to occupy the prophetic office. An example of a privilege is the ability to operate in certain gifts of the Holy Spirit without having desired it. First Corinthians 14:1 says to desire spiritual gifts, which suggest that to operate in any of the gifts mentioned in 1 Corinthians 12:1-10, it should be desired (although the Holy Spirit will appropriate it as He wills). Someone who is called to the prophetic office does not have to desire the gift of prophecy to operate in it. He manifests it automatically because it is a privilege that comes with the office. The reason for the privileges ascribed to this office is for the sole purpose of equipping the person to become successful in fulfilling the responsibilities of this office.

The office of the prophet was set by God to be one of His avenues of communicating to the church. Therefore, it has a responsibility of broadcasting what God is saying to the church, which the church may not be able to perceive otherwise. For this reason, the prophet is programmed to hear God for the people. It also helps the body of Christ to see where they may have gone wrong in their walk with God, so it can bring instructions, directions, corrections, and rebuke as directed by God.

Intercession

The prophetic office has a great responsibility of interceding for the body of Christ as well as for individuals. The importance of intercession cannot be overemphasized. Intercession is indeed one, if not the most important, task for the person called to this office. For this reason, the gift of diverse kinds of tongues is important in this ministry. When God gives a message to His prophets or prophetesses that involves something that will happen either in the future or now, the prophet's first reaction is to intercede for it. He prays to avert it if it is something bad or receive it if it is something good. In these circumstances, speaking in tongues is a very effective way of praying because the spirit of God prays through the person.

Sometimes God gives a prophet a word for someone, and He instructs the prophet not to tell the person the message but instead to intercede for that person. The prophet, therefore, must be prepared to embark on intercession and fasting for others, the body of Christ, and nations as the Holy Spirit leads. This is why all prophets are intercessors; although many prophets are not obedient to this aspect of their calling. Most prophets think that the scope of their calling only involves delivering a prophetic word. That is to declare only what God is telling the people. This is only a part of what this office entails. A true prophet must be an intercessor.

The Bible gives us some examples of prophets that interceded for the people in the Old Testament. Ezekiel 9 records that God was angry with the children of Israel because they said amongst themselves that God has forsaken the earth and that He does not see, so He sent His angels to separate the people into two sets. One set consisted of those who did not like the abomination in the land and did not keep silent about it. This set received a mark on their forehead that ensured their preservation. The other set consisted of those who did not fall within the first set, and they were to be destroyed. "And it came to pass, while they were slaying them, and I was left, that I fell upon my face, and cried, and said, 'Ah LORD God! wilt thou destroy all the residue of Israel in thy pouring out of thy fury upon Jerusalem?'" (Ezekiel 9:8).

The prophet Ezekiel immediately interceded for the people of Israel not to be destroyed. He could have said to himself, *God has already determined what to do to the people. Why pray for them anymore?* Even if his prayer might not change God's mind (which in fact it didn't), Ezekiel still prayed, just in case God would relent in His judgment.

Also, in Ezekiel 11, God was angry with the men that devised mischief amongst the people and gave wicked council. So Ezekiel was told to prophesy against the people.

> 'Ye have feared the sword; and I will bring the sword upon you, saith the LORD God. And I will bring you out of the mist thereof, and deliver you into the hands of strangers and will execute judgment among you. Ye shall fall by the sword; I will judge you in the border of Israel; and you shall know that I am the LORD. This city shall not be your caldron, neither shall you be the flesh in the mist thereof; but I will judge you in the border of Israel. And you shall know that I am the LORD: for you have not walked in my statutes, neither executed my judgments, but have done after the manner of the heathen that are round about you. And it came to pass, when I prophesied that Pelatiah the son of Benaiah died.' Then fell I down upon my face and cried with a loud voice and said, 'Ah LORD God! Wilt thou make a full end of the remnant of Israel?'
>
> Ezekiel 11:8-13

In this chapter, Ezekiel once again intercedes for the people of God, without allowing the prophetic word that he had just uttered stop him from praying and crying to God on behalf of the people. Ezekiel was definitely an intercessor.

The prophet Habakkuk also demonstrated that intercession was a great part of the prophetic ministry. Right from the beginning of chapter one and throughout all the other chapters, Habakkuk's passion for prayer is evident.

> The burden which Habakkuk the prophet did see. O LORD, how long shall I cry, and thou wilt not hear! even cry out unto thee of violence, and thou wilt not save!" Habakkuk 1:1-2

Habakkuk's approach to intercession throughout his book is one of dialogue between him and God. In chapter 1, he asked God a question, and God answered him in verses 3-10 of the same chapter. However, Habakkuk had a problem with this answer. You see unlike in the other cases where the prophets were interceding for God to have mercy on the people, Habakkuk's prayer was for God to bring judgment on the people, because of their evil practices. God heard his prayer but decided to punish the people through a nation worse off than them. This is what Habakkuk did not like. So he continued his dialogue with God in verse 12-17, appealing to God on why He should not use the evil nation to bring judgment. After pouring out his heart to God, he waited for an answer in chapter 2, which is as follows:

> I will stand upon my watch, and set me upon
> the tower, and will watch to see what he will
> say unto me, and what I shall answer when I
> am reproved.
>
> Habakkuk 2:1

It is important to note that as a child of God, you have the right to talk to your Father (God) in this same manner—where you can plead your case before Him. And as a prophet, you can dialogue with God in intercession, concerning a problem or burden that He may show you on behalf of the people. It does not matter if the case is for judgment or mercy. In fact, any true prophet who has been operating in this office for a while will testify that there have been times when they had to intercede for, or against, something on behalf of others or a course. This is one important marking of a true prophetic ministry where God speaks to the prophet about situations going on in and amongst His people. Some of the times when this happens, the prophet is not allowed to speak out what he or she has been told, instead it is for the prophet to bear a burden for that situation—to intercede for the problem or course in order for the people to receive the outcome that God wants.

God allows the prophet to bear a burden given to him spiritually, or He allows him to notice events happening around him in the natural that is not pleasing to God. These natural events also become burdens, just as in the case of Habakkuk with the sole purpose of birthing forth intercession in the prophet. That is one of the reasons why God told the prophet Ezekiel (3:17-21) that He has set him as a watchman over Israel to sound the alarm to the people. The alarm is to be sounded whether something good or bad is approaching the land. It is relevant to note that in sounding the alarm, God was not just referring to telling the people what was going to happen but also to be responsible for praying it to happen. Ezekiel was told that he would be held accountable for not warning the evil man of his ways. What exactly does this mean? It means that if God reveals what is in a person's heart to the prophet, and that it is evil, the prophet has the responsibility of first praying for that evil heart to change then delivering the message to the recipient if God's instruction is for that person to be told. Sometimes in intercessions like this, a dialogue can take place between the prophet and God. As he prays for the person, he can ask questions about whom he is praying for, and God answers. This can go on for a reasonable length of time.

Let us look at another prophet who also was a powerful intercessor, Abraham. His commitment to prayer saved the lives of his nephew Lot and his grand nieces from destruction in Sodom and Gomorrah. In this story, Abraham is seen conversing with God on behalf of the people in Sodom and Gomorrah. This is another example of how intercession can be done through a dialogue with God.

And the LORD said, because the cry of Sodom and Gomorrah is great, and because their sin is very grievous, I will go down now and see whether they have done altogether according to the cry of it, which is come unto me, and if not I will know. And the men turned their faces from thence and went toward Sodom: but Abraham stood yet before the LORD. And Abraham drew near and said, wilt thou also destroy the righteous with the wicked? Peradventure there be fifty righteous within the city: wilt thou also destroy and not spare the place for the fifty righteous that are therein? That be far from thee to do after this manner, to slay the righteous with the wicked: and that the righteous should be as the wicked, that be far from thee. Shall not the judge of all the earth do right?

Genesis 18:20-25

God answered Abraham.

And the LORD said, If I find in Sodom fifty righteous within the city, then I will spare all the place for their sakes.

Genesis 18:26

And Abraham answered and said, behold now, I have taken upon me to speak unto the LORD, which am but dust and ashes: Peradventure there shall lack five of the fifty righteous: wilt

thou destroy all the city for lack of five? And
he said, If I find there forty and five, I will not
destroy it.

Genesis 18:27-28

This dialogue between Abraham and God continued
for a while until Abraham stopped asking God. I wonder why he stopped, when he could have kept on asking God about the numbers and reducing it until it
got to one, or until God tells him to stop (the Bible
does not record that God told him to stop, it says that
God left after He finished talking with Abraham). It
is probable that if Abraham had reduced the number
of people to one, Sodom and Gomorrah might have
been spared, because Lot would have accounted for
that one person. Or, Abraham could have prayed after
he stopped counting, for some people to be able to perceive what God was going to do to the land.

It is my belief that if Abraham had prayed for
some people to somehow discern what God was about
to do in the land, instead of just pleading with God
not to destroy the people, more people might have
been saved, because some would have recognized the
angels or paid attention to what Lot was telling them,
thereby, responding to the call to leave the land. Well,
we will never know, will we? All I am trying to say is
that the prophet or anyone else for that matter should
never limit themselves in intercession. We should pray
every time and all angles. Listen to the leadership
of the Holy Spirit on how to direct the prayer, and

when the leading of the Holy Spirit is not sensed, pray from every point that we know naturally (your natural sense). The only exemption to this rule of praying from all angles and all that we know naturally is when God instructs us specifically not to pray or intercede as seen in Jeremiah.

The prophet Jeremiah was instructed by God not to pray for Israel. Yes! God was very clear on that word. The people did abominable works, and the house of God became a den of robbers. When God spoke to them to change, they did not listen nor heed. So God was angry and told Jeremiah not to intercede for the people for what He would do to them.

> And now, because ye have done all these works, saith the LORD, and I spake unto you, rising up early and speaking, but ye heard not; and I called you, but you answered not; Therefore will I do unto this house, which is called by my name, wherein ye trust, and unto the place which I gave to you and to your fathers, as I have done to Shiloh. And I will cast you out of my sight, as I have cast out all of your brethren, even the whole seed of Ephraim. Therefore, pray not for this people, neither lift up cry nor prayers for them, neither make intercession to me: for I will not hear thee.
>
> Jeremiah 7:13-16

The same instruction is also seen in Jeremiah 11:14. Here the people had broken God's covenant with them and had gone after other gods. So God told Jeremiah that He will bring evil upon them, and the people will not be able to escape. Jeremiah was forbidden to pray or intercede for the people. Another instance is found in Jeremiah 14:11 where he was asked not to pray for the people's good because of their iniquity. Therefore, in a situation where God clearly says, "Do not pray nor intercede," what is a prophet to do? The prophet is to obey God first and ask questions later. In other words, if you where at the point of intercession, and God gives you such direction, you are to leave that prayer point alone right there and pray for other things. That forbidden topic can be visited later with great wisdom. It is not that it will be a sin to ask God immediately why He does not want you to pray, because God will answer, or He will not—depending on how He wants it. But it is better to show obedience first. Addressing the matter later gives one time to pray and depend on the Holy Sprit on how to best approach the issue with God.

The question may be asked, if God instructs a person not to pray or intercede for something, will it not be wrong to ask God if we can pray? Or will it not be a sin to try to tell God why we should pray? The answer to these questions is no. An example of such circumstance is in Exodus 32. In this story, Moses went up to Mount Sinai to receive the Ten Commandments from God; Moses was delayed in his coming back, and the people (except a few) came together and built themselves a golden calf, which they worshipped as their god. Then the LORD said unto Moses, "I have seen these people, and, behold, it is a stiffnecked people: Now therefore let me alone, that my wrath may wax hot against them, and that I may consume them: and I will make of thee a great nation." (Exodus 32:9-10). When God said "Let Me alone," He was telling Moses not to plead (intercede) for the people. But Moses did not just let it go, the scriptures says that he besought God on their behalf with reasons why God should not destroy the people.

> And Moses besought the LORD and his God, and said, LORD, why doth thy wrath wax hot against thy people, which thou hast brought forth out of the land of Egypt with great power, and with a mighty hand? Wherefore should the Egyptians speak, and say, For mischief did he bring them out, to slay them in the mountains, and to consume them from the face of the earth? Turn from they fierce wrath, and repent of this evil against thy people. Remember Abraham, and Isaac, and Israel, thy servants, to whom thou swarest by thine own self, and saidst unto them, I will multiply your seed as the stars of heaven, and all this land that I have spoken of will I give unto your seed, and they shall inherit it for ever.
>
> Exodus 32: 11-13

Moses gave God reasons why he should not consume the people. The act of speaking to God on behalf of the people of course is intercession. So Moses found a way to pray for the people though God asked him to leave Him alone. This he did by bringing to God's remembrance His covenant with Israel. The Bible records that God relented of His plan to destroy them.

It was mentioned earlier that we are to obey and not pray right away if God instructs us not to. Apart from the obedience factor, we also see why it is wisdom to wait and ask God later about it, because it gives us time to be able to know which of God's words we are to bring back to Him concerning that situation, since God responds to His words. Although Moses interceded for the people right away, it is still better to obey first and ask questions later.

The importance of intercession in the prophetic ministry cannot be overemphasized. All prophets are intercessors. It is an intricate part of the ministry and the life of the prophet in order to successfully fulfill their assignments. A prophet or prophetess who is not prayerful has written him or herself a recipe for failure as a prophet and as a child of God. All over the scripture, all those called to this office are known to pray and intercede for others, thus the prophets today are to do likewise.

Prophetic Prayer

This is another type of prayer that is often seen in the prophetic office, although other people can also pray in this manner. It is important to note that prophetic prayer is more than praying scriptures over a situation. For example, if a person is sick, the Bible is opened, and Isaiah 53:4-5 is read to the sick person. To a degree this is prophetic praying; however, there is yet another level of prophetic prayer that a prophet can operate in by the leading of the Holy Spirit. This type of prayer can be a blessing or not depending on the situation and what needs to be done to rectify it. For instance, God told the prophet Ezekiel to prophesy against a forest. Yes, a forest, not a person.

> Son of man, set thy face toward the south, and drop thy word toward the south, and prophesy against the forest of the south field; and say to the forest of the south, Hear the word of the LORD; Thus saith the LORD God; Behold, I will kindle a fire in thee, and it shall devour every green tree in thee, and every dry tree: the flaming flame shall not be quenched, and all faces from the south to the north shall be burned therein.
>
> Ezekiel 20:46-48

On first examination of this scripture, it looks like Ezekiel was only prophesying because prophesy is God directly speaking His word to us. But what Ezekiel was really doing is prophetic praying.

In prophetic prayer, God tells us what to speak to a situation as we pray for that situation. God, in prayer, instructs or directs the person on what to do as he or she prays. This instruction or direction could be words or an action. In this case with Ezekiel, the instruction was for Ezekiel to drop his word. What word? The word he heard God say to him for the situation.

I remember one time a well-known preacher in Nigeria was asked to pray for a woman whose kids ran away from home; much praying had been done to no avail. As he started to pray, he stopped and called the father of the kids to place his hands on his wife's bosom, and the preacher placed his hands on that of the husband's. Then he said, "Except all of you did not suck out of this breast; if you did, then all of you will return to this breast from which you sucked." These children all returned home the next day after being away for a while. What happened to the children that made them to come home the very next day that did not happen before? Prophetic praying was done.

God gave the prophet instructions as he prayed on how to pray for that particular situation, and it yielded results immediately. Unlike the instruction given to Ezekiel when he prayed and spoke to the forest and dropped his words, this prophet of God had, in addition to speaking, an action. God told him to place his hands on the husband's hand. The husband then placed it on his wife's breast. I am sure that when the prophet did this, some people must have been shocked or confused as to what was happening. But when God instructs or directs in prophetic praying, it may not make sense sometimes.

I remember a time that I was called to pray for a woman who should be in labor, but the baby had not yet turned to the birthing position, and the doctor had

waited for about three days. The woman was sched-
uled to go for a cesarean section, and someone called
me to come and pray for her before she went to the
hospital. As I was praying for her, I heard the LORD
say to me to place her husband's hand on her stom-
ach and command the baby to turn. The next day, she
went to the hospital and the baby had already turned
to the birthing position. The doctors were amazed at
how quickly it had happened, and she gave birth to a
beautiful baby girl. I give God all the glory. Prophetic
prayer is very diverse in operation and is dependant on
the circumstances surrounding the problem.

There was a situation one time when our prayer
group in our ministry (God's Battle Axe Ministries)
was praying for the nations, and God instructed us to
turn and face the four corners of the earth and speak a
specific word to the nations and shout after the words
were spoken. Now this looks ridiculous to someone
who does not know or understand prophetic prayer.
In fact an example of a similar action is recorded in
scriptures.

> Now Jericho was straitly shut up because of
> the children of Israel: none went out, and none
> came in. And the LORD said unto Joshua, See, I
> have given into thine hand Jericho, and the king
> thereof, and the mighty men of valour. And ye
> shall compass the city, all ye men of war, and go
> round about the city once. Thus shalt thou do
> six days. And seven priests shall bear before the
> ark seven trumpets of ram's horn: and the sev-

enth day ye shall compass the city seven times, and the priests shall blow with the trumpets. And it shall come to pass, that when they make long blast with the ram's horn, and when ye hear the sound of the trumpet, all the people shall shout with a great shout; and the wall of the city shall fall down flat, and the people shall ascend up every man straight before him.

Joshua 6:1-5

What took place here was prophetic praying. God gave Joshua instructions on what to do and how to go about it. Prophetic prayer can be bizarre but yield great results when obeyed. So the next time you are praying concerning something and an instruction or direction on how you should pray comes to your mind, do not discard the thought except you are sure that it is not God speaking to you, because it may just be God telling you what to say and do. It may be time to prophetically pray.

THE GIFTS OF THE PROPHETIC OFFICE

There are different kinds of gifts that are in operation in the prophetic office. These gifts are made available by God through the Holy Spirit, and they are in this office for effective ministration. These gifts confer on the prophet or prophetess the ability to have the knowledge of things that are humanly impossible to know except revealed by God; hence they are called the revelational gifts. These gifts are word of wisdom and word of knowledge. In addition to these gifts is the gift of prophecy, which is paramount to this office. As the name implies, revelation means to reveal, disclose, bring out, broadcast, or to make known. It is important to note that other members of the body of Christ can and do operate in some or all of these gifts. However, the individual in the prophetic office should have all of the aforementioned gifts and be more frequent, accurate, and specific in their manifestations. There are other gifts that are at times evident in the prophetic office. However, it is not compulsory for the prophet to manifest them. These are discerning of spirits (a revelational gift), miracles, and healings.

The Bible records, in 1 Corinthians 12:7, the evidence of these gifts in the life of a believer is the manifestation of the Holy Spirit, and it is to profit all. It also clearly states in verse 11 that it is the same Holy Spirit that gives these gifts as needed. This means that a person can desire all or any one of them, the Holy Spirit is the one who will appropriate it as He wills. The question becomes: Why does the Holy Spirit not give every person every gift they ask for? The answer is found in the remaining verses of the book (12-31), which further explains that in the body of Christ there are many members, each with different purposes, passions, and callings. In other words, everybody cannot have exactly the same things (gifts) in the body, because only the same things will be done or fulfilled. Verse 17 emphasizes this point.

It is important to God that there are diverse gifts in the body, and this is why the Holy Spirit appropriates them as He wants. That way the work will be carried out effectively; for this reason, God has divinely allowed certain gifts to be made available to the different ministerial offices.

Therefore, we are to find out what our purpose, passion, or calling in the body is, and the gifts that rest upon that office will rest upon us. For the prophetic office, it is the revelational gifts and the gift of prophecy that all the prophets of old manifested throughout their ministries. They were also evident in the ministry of Jesus, as well as other people in the New Testament. The importance of these gifts in this office cannot be overemphasized, especially in the area of intercession. What makes a prophet more effective in intercession is his/her ability to hear and to see in the spirit realm.

The way by which the prophet hears and sees in the spirit realm is through these gifts, which are operative by dreams, visions, or hearing the Word of God in your spirit or even audibly. The ability of the prophet to manifest these gifts is quite simple because it is dependant on the Holy Spirit. I found that the word of knowledge and wisdom can be received through dreams and visions as well as by unction, while the gift of prophecy—most of the time—is by unction. Prophecy is kind of in a class of its own when compared to the word of wisdom and knowledge. It is vast and a little more complicated because it has so many facets. It is also the most common and certainly the most misunderstood and abused of all the gifts.

The Word of Wisdom

The word of wisdom is better explained by an illustration. In one prophetic meeting in September of 2007, the LORD showed me a gunman, and the word that followed was that the enemy was planning an attack on school children. We were to cancel such an attack from happening, because it would be bloody and worse than the Columbine school shootings. We were not told the name of the school, nor did God say the county or state. It was a word given, and an action was needed.

We prayed about this at that meeting and canceled every plan of the enemy. Less than a week later, a gunman went to Delaware University and shot some people. You might ask, if God said pray against it, why then did it still happen? Believe me when I say that is the same question I asked God, and His answer was; it was not worse than the Columbine shootings because all of you prayed. What do you say after that? He is God, and He has the last word. *But I thought that to prophesy was to edify and lift up, never to condemn, or cause fear?* you might ask. My answer to that question is that this was a word of wisdom, not prophecy. You see the word of wisdom is not given to edify; it is given to warn one of an imminent or distant danger or to take caution in making a decision. It is supposed to help the believer not to make a mistake or walk into an adverse situation without knowing. For too long the church has classified every word spoken by God through His prophets as prophecy alone, hence the confusion in the body of Christ.

What is the gift of the word of wisdom? This is not to be mistaken with regular wisdom. The word "regular" is used here to distinguish it from the gift of the word of wisdom. "Regular" wisdom as defined by Webster's dictionary and thesaurus is the quantity of being wise; good judgment; learning; knowledge; experience; clear thinking; understanding; and having common sense, to mention a few. This type of wisdom, simply put, is the ability to make right decisions.

A biblical example is King Solomon in 1 King 3. In this chapter, Solomon asks the LORD for wisdom to rule his nation in making judgment between right and wrong. As Christians, we are supposed to pray and know when to make the right decisions for the people we are responsible for and ourselves. This type of wisdom is available to all who seek God's counsel about anything.

The gift of the word of wisdom is similar to regular wisdom in that it also involves making decisions but yet different because the person operating this gift is giving a word of warning about something that will happen in the future. God may give the speaker the word for him or herself or for someone else. The key point in operating the word of wisdom is that the individual is speaking concerning something he or she does not know about because it has not yet occurred; it is futuristic. To the recipient, the word of wisdom comes to help them make a better decision about that futuristic event or incident.

Most of the time, the word of wisdom will have enough information to require the right decision to be made if the people hearing the word believe and receive it; the decision may need to be made immediately or not. Some examples of where the word of wisdom is seen in scriptures are found in Isaiah 7:14-15, 9:6-7, and 11:1-5. These scriptures foretell the coming of the Messiah who is Jesus the Christ. It was a word of wisdom to the Jews when it was told to them before the coming of Christ. It was a warning of what will happen in the future, so that when Christ comes, they will know to make a decision to follow Him. Praise God that now the word has come to pass, for Christ has already come and He will come back again.

Another example of this gift is also seen when the prophet Jonah was sent to Nineveh to inform the people that they would be destroyed in forty days. This is word of wisdom in operation because it required the people to make a decision about a futuristic event or face the consequences. The people, knowing that God is good—I believe from what they have heard about Him—repented immediately and were spared (Jonah 3:3-10).

It is important to note that sometimes the decision to be made may not necessarily be the right or wrong decisions, but the "God" decision, even if it seems wrong to man. In making this type of decisions, the people or person involved must be sure that they have heard from God. An example of such is in the case of Apostle Paul in Acts 21:10-11. In this instance, God sent the prophet Agabus to him, and the word of wisdom was that Paul would be bound in chains by the Jews in Jerusalem and he would be delivered to the Gentiles. Note that God did not send Agabus to tell Paul not to go, just what will happen when he goes. The action Paul was to take was entirely up to him. Paul made the "God" decision, and he went to Jerusalem. How do we know that this decision was the one that was God's will? Because in Acts 21:13, Paul said that he was ready to be bound and die in Jerusalem for the name of the LORD Jesus. This means that he suspected or knew what would happen to him if he went to Jerusalem, or he just did not care what would happen as long as he was preaching the gospel. You see Paul knew that he would suffer many things for the gospel (Acts 9:15-16), so if to be bound and die was part of that suffering, then he was ready to die for what he believed. His going to Jerusalem, therefore, became the right decision because it was the "God" decision.

In ministry as a prophetess, God has sent me several times with a word of wisdom to different people. Once I was sent to give a word to a man of God. The word was for him to pray in order to stop the devil's plan of tampering with their place of worship. God wanted him to remain at a certain place for a time, then He would take him somewhere else, to a much better place. This word was perceived as false because he wanted to move, so the word was not *encouraging* to him, and as such he felt it could not be from God. But the word of God came to pass not long from the day that it was spoken. The problem in this scenario was that the man of God felt that the word given to him was a prophecy and as such should encourage him. The word however was not from the gift of prophecy; instead it was a word of wisdom. God was warning him of the intent of the devil concerning his place of worship, and it required him to make a decision—a decision to pray and avert it or not to pray and let it happen. When God gives us a word through His prophets or anyone who operates the gifts of the prophetic ministry, we should not be too quick to judge the person because the word does not sound like what we want. It might not be a prophecy; it may be a word of wisdom. So spend a moment to analyze and pray about it and see if it requires a decision to be made. Then allow the Holy Spirit to help you make the "God" one.

The Word of Knowledge

The word *knowledge* means to know. Webster's dictionary describes it as "a state of knowing; the body of facts accumulated by mankind; range of information or understanding." Here the dictionary meaning clearly emphasizes the fact that something is known. The question is, what is known? The answer to this is information, which was acquired over time either by reading or listening. As Webster rightly puts it, "facts accumulated by mankind." It denotes something you already knew about, concerning a subject matter; this is knowledge. On the contrary, the gift of the word of knowledge as given by the Holy Spirit does not depend on accumulated knowledge. That is, it does not have anything to do with what you have studied or listened to over time; rather, it is total dependence on the Holy Spirit to tell you in an instance what has happened over time or what is happening now either to a person a place. The word of knowledge, therefore, is the ability to know what a person has done in the past or doing right now without having been told before then. There are several examples recorded in the Bible of where this gift was used, however, only a few are written in this book.

There is an interesting story in 1 Samuel 15:3 where God told Saul through the prophet Samuel to kill all the Amalekites, including women, children, and animals. The story continues in verse 9 that Saul spared Agag, the king, and the best of the sheep and oxen, as well as the fatlings and the lambs. Saul did not totally destroy the Amalekites as God instructed him. It is important to note that the prophet Samuel did not go to war with King Saul; neither did someone tell him what happened at war. The Bible says that God told Samuel what Saul did (1 Samuel 15:10-14). Wow! Samuel knew what Saul had done because God told him. In the same way, a person who has this gift has information about something he does not know anything about because the Holy Spirit tells him or her.

The prophet Nathan was also told by God what he did not know anything about in 2 Samuel 12:1-10. In this story, King David had seduced Bathesheba, the wife of Uriah, who was one of his soldiers, and had gotten her pregnant. He then tried to cover up his folly, and when that did not work out, King David had Uriah killed. Then God sent Nathan to chastise David for what he had done. Nathan was made privy to a secret that had occurred in the palace, knowing this secret is by the word of knowledge. Remember that this is the ability to know what has happened or is happening without being told by anyone or seen by you.

It is important to emphasize that the scenario of Nathan with David also portrays how a prophet can deliver a word of knowledge, wisdom, or even prophecy in the form of a parable. God would use any means or format that will be more receptive or explanatory to bring a message to His people. I believe that in the case of David, a parable was the better format for him to really see what he had done and how bad it was. So it should not be a surprise to a Christian when God speaks to us in parables through His prophets. In whatever situation that this occurs, God will also bring the interpretation or the understanding either to the person receiving the word or to the prophet who is giving it.

The examples that have been studied thus far about this gift are all in the Old Testament. Though, at the time it was not referred to as the word of knowledge, the principle by which these prophets had their information is the same. Now let us study some examples of this gift being used in the New Testament.

The LORD Jesus Christ exhibited this gift in His ministry while He was on earth. An appropriate scenario is the discussion that transpired between Jesus and the Samaritan woman who met Him at the well in John 4:16-19. Jesus asked her to give Him water to drink, and the woman wondered why a Jew would ask anything from a Samaritan. One conversation led to another and Jesus eventually sent her on an errand. He told her, "Go, call your husband and come back."

"I have no husband," she replied.

Jesus said to her, "You are right when you say you have no husband. The fact is, you have had five husbands, and the man you now have is not your husband."

"What you have just said is quite true, sir," the woman said. "I can see that you are a prophet," the woman concluded.

The woman concluded that Jesus was a prophet because she knew without a doubt that the only way He was aware of her life history was by supernatural means. Jesus knew all about the woman's past and present by the gift of the word of knowledge.

We might say, "This is Jesus! Of course He knew. He knows all things." It is true that Jesus knows all things; however, when Jesus was here on earth, He was all man as well as God. Everything He knew or did was by the ability of the Holy Ghost. In like manner, Christians have the same ability to walk in these gifts because God the Father has bestowed it upon us through the Holy Spirit, because of the redemptive work of Jesus Christ on the cross. Furthermore, Jesus said that we would do greater works than He did. Jesus is the Son of God, but He also was a prophet when He was on earth. And now His prophetic side has been given to the church in the office of a prophet, which as we know is one of the five-fold ministry gifts of Jesus.

The application of this gift is very vast comprising of different circumstances and not limited to places, time, or people. It is noteworthy that this gift is also at work when an infirmity is revealed to a minister without him having a fore knowledge of it.

The Gift of Prophecy

This is one of the most common of the gifts in the prophetic office, yet it is the most confusing to a lot of people. The church has over the years attributed every spoken word from the mouth of prophets to the gift of prophecy; whereas there is the word of wisdom and knowledge. Indeed prophecy means to speak forth or to declare God's word, which in a broad sense makes it relative to word of wisdom and knowledge or, anytime a scripture is read over a situation. The gift of prophecy, however, is slightly different from prophecy itself. Let me explain. Any believer can prophesy as long as they are declaring God's word either to themselves or a situation. In this regard, everyone is a prophet unto him or herself. The Bible teaches us that the man is the head of his household. Therefore, when a man declares God's promises over his family, he is prophesying to them. In this way every believer can and should prophesy over their lives and declare what belongs to them. But the gift of prophecy is different. A person who operates in this gift does not just declare the written word of God alone over himself, herself, or a situation that he or she finds himself or herself in, but they also divinely hear from God specifics, as it relates to whatever issue the LORD wants to communicate expressly to other people individually, or to the church at large.

It is important to note that it is not everyone who operates in the gift of prophecy that has the mantle or is in the office of a prophet. The father who declares scriptures over his household is a prophet to his own house; it does not necessarily mean that he is called to occupy the prophetic office. While the person whom God has called and raised to function in the prophetic office is a prophet, not just to his household, but to the church in which they are ordained and to the body of Christ in general. It is important to note that prophets are not ordained to a single church. God alone calls anyone in the five-fold ministry, and they have a purpose in the body of Christ. Of course that minister has a responsibility to his local assembly; however, it goes beyond their local assembly to the body in general. It happens that the ordination for service has to take place somewhere. So God allows a church to recognize the call in people as they continue to serve in their local assemblies and uses that assembly to ordain them. The church needs to get past the animosity and divisions that exists among ministers in claiming ownership over people, embrace one another in their respective callings, and perform the task that is set before us in the vineyard of God.

The Gift of Discerning of Spirits

Another gift of the spirit in the prophetic office that should be seen in all five-fold ministry, but rarely observed in the body today is the discernment of spirits. What exactly is the discernment of spirits? This has been defined in many different ways. It has been said to be the ability to see demonic spirits in people as well as in the atmosphere. Others have defined it as not just the ability to see demons but also to see angels and the heavenly host. In a way they are both correct because it does involve the ability to see spirit beings, whether demonic or angelic. However, it is much more than these definitions.

One major way that the discernment of spirits should be in operation is in a situation where the truth of God's word has been deliberately masked. That is a lie that has been perpetuated as God's truth, or the truth has been mixed with lies for self-gain, image, money, or other dubious means. The most common example of this gift in the church today is the ability to identify someone operating in familiar spirits. That is witchcraft, occultism, and seducing spirits, to mention a few. Unfortunately, the church has relegated the operation of this gift to these aspects alone rather than embrace it in all of its totality. In fact this gift has caused a lot of breakups and trouble in the body of Christ, because of lack of understanding. If there is a gift most perverted, it is this one. Many people have accused others wrongly of seducing (Jezebel) spirits because they supposedly discerned the spirit. The church has reduced this gift to name calling and witch hunting. Indeed the ability to discern familiar spirits is a part of this gift, but what a small part it is in its otherwise vast manifestations.

This gift is supposed to help, the body of Christ stay on course in our day-to-day activities as Christians in the doctrine of the Bible. As was mentioned before, that means, when a doctrine or practice that is not scriptural creeps up, the church body should be able to discern it as false by the operation of this gift. That is why it is important for the people in leadership to have it. Let us consider an example of this gift in operation. The book of Acts 8:9-24 has a very interesting story about a man called Simon, a sorcerer in Samaria. The story reveals that this man heard the gospel through Phillip and accepted Jesus as his savior. He even got baptized and continued with Phillip, beholding all the signs and miracles that God performed through him. The story records that when the apostles in Jerusalem heard what was been done in Samaria—that the people had received the gospel—they sent Peter and John to them, who laid hands on the converts to receive the Holy Ghost. When Simon, the former sorcerer saw this, he wanted a piece of the action. He wanted to be able to lay his hands on the people also so that they will receive the Holy Ghost. This in itself was not wrong; the only problem was that he offered money for it. In his offering money for receiving the anointing for the laying on of hands, he thought that he could bribe or buy God, which means that he had not yet completely denounced his old ways. You see in his old ways, he practiced his acts for money, and if he were to receive the anointing, he will take money from people before he prayed for them.

This Peter could tell by discerning Simon's spirit that the reason he wanted the anointing was wrong— it was for selfish purposes. That is why verses 22-23 of the same chapter records:

> Repent therefore of this thy wickedness, and
> pray God, if perhaps the thought of thine heart
> may be forgiven thee. For I perceive that thy
> art in the gall of bitterness, and in the bond of
> iniquity.

The Apostle Peter said that he perceived; that means that he sensed, or better still, that he discerned what Simon was really about. You might ask, what if Simon offered money out of ignorance? Well, if it were out of ignorance, then Peter would simply have explained the appropriate way of receiving the anointing rather than scolding him on the error of his ways. After all, in the day of ignorance God overlooks, the scripture says (Acts 17:30). Therefore, God would have made Peter handle the situation differently if ignorance was Simon's problem.

Another example of this gift in operation is also in the book of Acts 17:16-23. Here, the Apostle Paul was in Athens, and verse 17 says that his spirit was stirred up when he saw the city wholly given to idolatry. Anyone conversant with the operations of the Holy Spirit would understand that God was up to something for the people of Athens hence the stirring up of Paul's spirit by the Holy Ghost. So his spirit was stirred up, and he went about doing that which he does the most, preaching the gospel. Then the people of the city brought him unto Areopagus, wanting to know the new doctrine that he was preaching (You see, the people of Athens were very knowledgeable and loved philosophy). Then Paul said to then in verse 22b, "Ye men of Athens, I perceive that in all things ye are too superstitious."

It is important to note that Paul did not say in this thing (that would mean he was referring to the preaching of the gospel to the Athenians) you are superstitious. Rather, he said in all things, which means that Paul knew their nature (the nature of a person is in his spirit, it is who he really is), was to be superstitious no matter what they heard. Paul was able to discern what their mindset was. If Paul knew this fact based on history or any other natural means, he would not have used the word *perceive*, instead he would have said, "I know." Please note that I am not saying every time a person perceives something, that it is the discernment of spirits gift in operation. Instead, I am saying that this gift can sometimes be active in perception. As seen in the case of Paul, there was a stirring in his spirit before this story unfolded, and at the end of it, the gospel was preached, souls were won, and God took the glory.

In another city during one of Paul's missionary journeys, the need for this gift arose (Acts 16:16-18). It was when a demon-possessed girl told the crowd that Paul was preaching to, to hear him. Paul rebuked the girl and commanded the demon spirit to leave her. The interesting part of this story is that the girl followed Paul to places in the city that he preached in for many days before she was rebuked. Two questions come to mind. One is, why did Paul rebuke the girl? After all, she was saying a good thing—which is supposed to make Paul's preaching job easier—by telling the people, her people, to listen to Paul. And the second question is, why was she not rebuked immediately when she began to follow Paul? The answer to the first is that Paul rebuked her because she was practicing divination, which is against God's rule; and the answer to the second question is this: it is probable that Paul did not realize the spirit the girl had from the beginning on time. If Paul had known from the beginning of her following him, he would have rebuked her earlier. So how did Paul know? By the gift of discernment, that's how. I believe that Paul did not tap into the gift immediately, but he eventually did, and the girl was delivered in the name of Jesus. This is a very good example of a situation where the gift of discernment is needed. In the body of Christ today, the spirit of divination is still at work, but the sad thing is that we are not able to discern it in most cases.

The discernment of spirits can also be used to tell what someone is thinking about. Please note that the practice of mind reading through any medium is a sin and is not what I am referring to in this category. It is important that we understand that the ability of some prophets or believers to tell what a person is thinking is given by the Holy Ghost alone, to serve whatever purpose that the LORD wants at that particular time. And it is not to be equaled or confused with mind reading. Most of the time when a prophet is able to tell what is on someone's mind, he or she does not know at that time what he is hearing in the spirit is the other person's thoughts. He only knows when the recipient of the word given confirms that what was just said was what he was thinking.

I remember one prophetic conference that I attended some years ago. At this meeting, the prophet called me out and said that I knew better than to be at the church where I was worshipping at that time, and the LORD used him to give me reasons why I should have known better. Then I said in my mind, *But God, You know I am in the process of leaving now*, and the prophet said to me, "Why did it take you this long?" If that is not scary, then I do not know what is. God answered my unspoken question right there through the same person.

This man did not know me or know of me. Yet he first chastised me by the word of knowledge and then answered my question by discerning what was in my spirit. What a mighty God we serve. This prophet did not even know that he had answered my unspoken question by the spirit of God, because I never told him.

I have sometimes found myself in these situations where God has used me to answer other people's unspoken question. There was one meeting that we had where God gave me a word for a pastor. I gave the word and kept on preaching. Then I heard the Holy Spirit speaking to me about the same pastor I just gave a word to. I stopped preaching and delivered what I was told. I continued preaching again, and had to stop to deliver another word. At the end it was a total of four times I had to stop to say what God was telling me to, to this same person.

At a point, I thought I was wrong or missing it somehow. By the third time the Holy Spirit spoke to me concerning this same person, I prayed and said, "God, please do not let me hear myself." But I continued to give the messages, because I was convinced that it was God. I am sure that some people felt that I was picking on this pastor or something. As God would have it, before the end of the meeting, this pastor asked if she could say something, and she came to the front of the congregation and began to cry and say that God loves her so much. She said all the questions that she asked God in her heart while I was preaching, God answered through me. Praise God. You see if she did not tell us that all the words that came forth were God's replies to her, I, along with everybody else, would never have known what had transpired between her and God. Now let us take a biblical example of this gift.

There is this story where Jesus was invited by a Pharisee to come to eat at his house in Luke 7:36-50. The story narrates that a certain woman who was a prostitute came to Jesus in the house of Simon the Pharisee to meet Jesus. She washed His feet with her tears and wiped it with her hair. Then she broke her alabaster box of precious ointment and anointed His feet after she had kissed them. Verse 39 says that when the Pharisee who invited Jesus saw what the prostitute did, he said within himself (in his thoughts) "This man, if He were a prophet, would have known who and what manner of woman this is that toucheth Him: for she is a sinner."

Then Jesus answered his thoughts with a parable. It is evident that Jesus heard Simon's unspoken words, because He answered them. What enabled Jesus to know Simon's thoughts was the gift of discernment.

The discernment of spirits can also be used to remember a dream. Some reader might ask the question, what is the correlation between remembering a dream and discerning of spirits? There is indeed a correlation. When a person is dreaming, all the activities that occur are not in a natural state, it is in an unseen realm: the spirit realm. No matter how real the dream seems, when we wake up, it is no longer there, because it all happened in the spirit realm. Therefore, the ability of a person to remember any dream is a very small measure of the gift of discernment in operation. God has given this measure to all human beings. However, there is a greater measure that operates in some people. This is the ability to know a dream not dreamt by you, neither was it told to you as in the case of Daniel.

The book of Daniel 2 gives us a good example of this level of discernment of spirits. The story records that King Nebuchadnezzar had a dream, and that when he woke up, he forgot what the dream was. He, however, knew that it was important for him to know what the dream entailed. He then called all of his magicians, sorcerers, and astrologers who were part of his wise men to come and tell him what he had dreamt. But to no avail, none could tell the king what he wanted to know. So the king ordered the death of the wise men, of which Daniel was amongst them. Daniel went to the king and begged for time to see if he could tell the king what he so desired.

It is important to note that it was not the interpretation of the dream that the king demanded, but the dream itself. So in other for anyone to know this, they have to be able to have the same dream the king dreamt, or be able to see into the king's spirit and discern what is inside. Either way, the spirit realm had to be tapped into. Because the beginning of the story says that King Nebuchadnezzar's spirit was so troubled that his dream broke from him. The emphasis here is that it was his spirit and not his mind that was troubled while he dreamed. He was so troubled that he abruptly came out of the spiritual realm and lost his dream. The dream was, therefore, locked up inside his spirit. This is why nobody could tell it. It was easier a task, and more common to interpret a dream rather than recapture one. For this reason, the Chaldeans answered the king saying:

"And it is a rare thing that the king requireth, and there is none other that can shew it before the king, except the gods, whose dwelling is not with flesh" (Daniel 2:11).

Daniel, in asking for time from the king, certainly had a hard task ahead of him. He had to be able to know that particular dream that was locked up in the king's spirit. But, just as the Chaldeans reply was to the king, Daniel did the same thing. The difference was that he sought the God of heaven and earth, who revealed it to him in a night vision (dream). What this means is that God played the dream that the king had to Daniel, He allowed Daniel discern in the spirit realm King Nebuchadnezzar's dream. This degree of discernment of spirit is rare today in the church although it is still operative. I remember a meeting that I attended in 2008, where a prophet told a woman in detail the dream she had some time ago. The woman agreed that the prophet was right. She was prayed for after the prophet told her the meaning of her dream, and God delivered her that day.

The Gift of Miracles and Healings

The prophetic ministry also has the gift of faith, working of miracles, and gift of healings attached to its office. However, not all prophets operated in these gifts in the Old Testament, and the same is true today in the body of Christ. Indeed all believers have the ability to call forth healing and miracles by faith in the name of the LORD Jesus, but the gift of faith, healing, and the working of miracles as seen in 1 Corinthians 12:9-10 is operated differently. By this I mean that a prophet or anyone who has any of these gifts bestowed unto them, manifest them only by the unction of the Holy Spirit at certain times. Just like prophecy or the word of knowledge comes by unction of the Holy Ghost as God allows, so does the manifestations of the aforementioned gifts. Anyone who has these gifts known as the power gifts, knows when the unction is on them to manifest it as well as when the unction lifts.

In view of the preceding paragraph, let us consider an example in other to understand better. I once heard a popular minister who has these power gifts say that he had a crusade where a lot of people were on the line to be ministered to for different healing. The minister said that as he continued to pray for the people, there were miracles and instant manifestations of healings. Then it came to a point when he felt that the unction to minister in that capacity lifted from him, but then there was this boy who wanted to be healed. So he told him that right now, he was tired, and he really did not know if the boy would be healed or not because the anointing (for the gift of healings) had lifted. However, he prayed for the boy in faith in the name of Jesus. Nothing happened after he prayed, but he found out later that the boy got healed. Now the difference between when he ministered in the power gifts and when he prayed in faith in the name of Jesus is that, while he ministered in the power gifts, God did not necessarily require the faith of either the minister or the recipient in other for there to be a manifestation. It totally depended on God's mercy and grace.

As was mentioned before, not all prophets have the power gifts. The prophets that do have them are not more important than those who do not. It is only a matter of differences in assignments. For example, the prophets Elijah, Elisha, and Moses had signs, miracles, and healings in their ministries, while Jeremiah,

Ezekiel, and Isaiah did not. Of course it is known that not one is higher or greater than another. In fact, the prophet John in the New Testament, who did no miracles nor signs and wonders, was called greater than all the Old Testament prophets by Jesus. So what matters as a prophet or a minister is not the different gifts that we manifest, although it is important. Instead to be successful in our God-given assignment is more excellent.

Non-personal Prophecies

The question do all prophecies come to pass is pivotal to the understanding of the prophetic office and needs to be addressed. Although it looks simple, unfortunately it has been of great contradiction and a stumbling block to the prophetic office. Many people say if a prophet gives you a word of prophecy, then that word must come to pass if it is of God, especially when a time, place, season, name, or other very definite specifics are said.

The prophet that prophesies this very specific word is termed *false* if these predictions do not come to pass, or if they do come to pass but not exactly as he or she had spoken. Before I go further to deal with this question, I would like to clarify that I am not saying that a specific word given by a prophet does not have to happen exactly as it was said. Instead, what

I am trying to communicate is that there are many factors that affect and propel prophecies to happen or not. These factors are dependant on the recipient most of the time and sometimes on the environment. Prophecies—I believe—can be classified into two parts; I choose to call it non-personal or non-individual prophecy and personal or individual prophecies.

Non-personal prophecies are those that God has given that have nothing to do with the personal gratification or fulfillment of individualistic plan and purpose.

> We have also a more sure word of prophecy; whereunto ye do well that ye take heed, as unto a light that shineth in a dark place, until the day dawn, and the day star arise in your hearts: Knowing this first, That no prophecy of the scripture is of any private interpretation.
>
> 2 Peter 1:19-20

What this means is that there are prophecies given that are not meant to change, enhance, or promote our personal lives directly. That is the prophecy was not given to and for one person to benefit from; for example, they are not prophecies to get a house, get a car, find a husband, expand a business, answer prayers, answer questions, or meet expectations. Rather they are prophecies that God has spoken to improve, enhance, and promote His plan with mankind in general. Such prophecies are to impact nations, deliver people, and bring redemption and insight.

These non-personal prophecies are not dependant on human factors or environmental conditions. They are one hundred percent dependent on God and will come to pass no matter what. So do all non-personal prophecies come to pass? Yes, all of these non-personal prophecies will come to pass, only due to the fact that it has nothing to do with man's cooperation. Some examples of such prophecies are the birth of the Messiah and His ministry. Other examples are the prophetic words given to Paul that he would impact the gentiles, Jonah told to go to Nineveh, the birth of John told to Zachariah, the ministry of John the Baptist, the birth of Samson told to Manoah and his wife, Israel's coming back from captivity in Babylon, the exodus from Egypt, the promise of David's son to sit on the throne forever, to mention a few.

The question one might ask here is if these prophecies are one hundred percent dependant on God, why then do people play a part in them? The answer to this question is people play a part because God works through people. However, in the case of these prophecies, the people involved had no choice in the matter. That is the prophecies will and did come to pass, whether they liked it or not and whether they were willing participant from the onset or not. In cases like these, if the people involved are not willing at first, God would process the person by allowing them to go through some things, which could be good or bad situations as the case may be until the people comply.

One way in which God does this is to change the comfortable circumstance around the person. He or she can be displaced from his or her environment until he or she becomes a willing participant. God will not force His will on anyone, but can make the person's will become His own. Such a person whom God uses to fulfill such prophecies, were born for this reason: to be a vehicle that God wants to use to bring to pass certain things. It is their assignment in life, their destiny to help propagate God's plan and purpose for mankind. For this reason, prophecies given about such people always come to pass. These non-personal prophecies are divided into two sub divisions: attached and non-attached.

Non-personal and Non-attached Prophecies

This is an example of a non-personal prophecy, but this type is not attached to anyone. These are prophecies that are released into the atmosphere that may determine major or minor events, but does not have its fulfillment attached to anyone in particular. When it is the time or season for such prophecies to be manifested, God uses whoever he wants to fulfill His will. It is important to note that the person may not know until the time for the prophecy to be fulfilled. Let us examine such a situation. The prophecy about the Messiah was given many years before it was fulfilled. Mary the mother of Jesus did not know until the time the angel visited her that she was the one to bear the

Holy Child. The gospel according to St. Luke 1:26-35 records this story.

Then said Mary unto the angel, "How shall this be, seeing I know not a man?"

The angel's reply in the next verse was

> And the angel answered and said unto her, the Holy Ghost shall come upon thee, and the power of the Highest shall overshadow thee: therefore also that holy thing which shall be born of thee shall be called the Son of God.

In these verses, it is evident that Mary never knew before the day that the angel visited her that she would give birth to the Messiah. Although it was common knowledge in Israel that the Messiah would come and that His mother would be a virgin, these prophecies were, however, spoken into the atmosphere (non-attached) and not once was Mary or any other woman's name mentioned as the mother. Let us examine one of the prophecies that stated that a virgin would give birth. The Prophet Isaiah in chapter 7 verse 14 declared that a virgin shall conceive and give birth to a son. Isaiah was probably perceived as crazy, eccentric, or maybe drunk at the utterance of this prophecy. If this prophecy were given in this century, people would frown on it even with the advancement of technology and science not to talk of in the days of the Old Testament. A virgin giving birth, how ridiculous it must have seemed.

All manner of things might have been said because the people could not understand or see the possibility of this happening. The interesting fact is that this prophecy came to pass, whether the people believed it or not. Why did it come to pass? Because it was one hundred percent dependant on God, therefore, man could not have stopped it. This prophecy was about a major event that would change and save mankind; that would reconcile the world back to God, to fulfill God's sovereign plan on earth, and as such it was non-personal. It was for everyone and all. Although it took many years for it to happen, it did. At God's appropriate time, He looked for a vessel to use, and it was made manifest.

In the story of the birth of Jesus, it is known that Mary was a willing participant from the beginning and that Joseph was not until later. Mary could have refused to be the mother to bare our LORD Jesus, but she obeyed regardless of the persecution she knew she would face. Joseph in contrast did not believe at first, (which is understandable considering the fact that he did not initially see the angel who appeared to Mary) but later he believed. The point here is that non-personal prophecies will always come to pass, no matter how long it takes or how willing or unwilling the people are or become.

Another example in this category of prophecies is the prophetic word given by the prophet Hosea. In Hosea 11:1, the prophet declared by the word of God that God's son would be called out of Egypt. Now, the question is which of God's sons? Is it Israel or Jesus? Since Exodus 4:22-23 address Israel as God's first son. Here again we see a non-attached prophecy. The book of Matthew 2:13-15 (the coming back of Joseph with his family from his escape to Egypt) is what later gave clarification to this prophetic manifestation, because it emphasizes that this scripture is a fulfillment of a prophecy. Therefore, Hosea's message was a prophecy about our LORD Jesus.

Jesus then had to be taken to Egypt one way or another in order for Hosea's prophecy to come to pass. It was unfortunate though that the event that led to the fulfillment of this word was a sad one, because babies and toddlers were killed. We know that God did not instruct Herod to kill the young children and the babies, rather He allowed the situation, and used it to bring His word to pass, as it must. Matthew 2:13-14 says that an angel warned Joseph by night to take the young child and His mother to Egypt, because the king wanted to destroy Him. Also, Joseph was instructed to stay in Egypt until God brought him word to leave. Joseph was later told to leave Egypt with his family and go back to Israel because the danger was over (Matthew 2:19-20).

In this story, the hand of God alone in bringing this prophecy by Hosea to pass is very evident. Joseph and Mary had no part to play in orchestrating all the circumstances that led to their departure from Bethlehem to Egypt. In other words, God knows and will do exactly what is necessary to make sure that prophecies that are non-personal are fulfilled. Another of such example is that of John the Baptist. The Prophet Malachi in 3:1 and 4:5-6 declared by the spirit of the LORD that a messenger (no name) shall come and prepare the way of the LORD. He also said that the prophet Elijah (named, but it was obvious that Elijah was dead) would come before the last days. These prophecies are reconciled in Luke 1:11-17 and 76-77. It is seen that John the Baptist is that prophet, not Elijah coming personally, but John in the spirit of Elijah (this is an example where a prophecy may not happen as you think it should), he was to be the one to prepare the way for the LORD's coming. When the initial prophecy was given in Malachi, it was not given to anyone in particular (non-attached). When it was time for its manifestation, God chose a family, which everyone can testify that God alone brought the prophecy to pass since Elizabeth was not only barren, but was past childbearing age, and her husband was equally old. A non-personal, non-attached prophecy released into the atmosphere, will—in due season by God's hand alone—be fulfilled through whom He has prepared for it.

Non-personal prophecies are still spoken even in these days that we are in. For example, if you attend a prophetic meeting or a Christian gathering where there were prophecies spoken, not to a particular person, but to everyone present about what God is doing or will do in the future. Such prophecies are declared into the atmosphere, and, at the appropriate time, they are fulfilled through the vessels that God chooses. The people whom God uses may or not have attended the meetings in which the prophecies were given. You hear prophets and other ministers declaring what God is doing or will do on the earth in the near future. Although many people take these words lightly and do not think much of them, it does not nullify the truth that God still speaks in this manner and they are being fulfilled.

Other examples of God's prophetic words are those heard usually at the end or beginning of a new year. Many ministers wait on the LORD to hear what He will say to His people in the new year, hence you hear things like 2007, the year of divine grace and prosperity, or 2008, the year of God's favor, open doors, etc. These words are spoken by God to all. Those who will hear and believe it, will see them manifest in different areas. The manifestation for one may be different from that of another and sometimes, such words come to pass even in areas where there were no expectations for it, and so we may not realize that they had happened. But they did.

Non-personal Attached Prophecies

This is another example of a non-personal prophecy, but unlike the non-attached, which is spoken into the atmosphere, this type of prophecy is attached. By attached I mean it is given specifically to someone or a people or a place. Remember, it is non-personal, and so undermining the fact that it is attached it is still one hundred percent dependent on God alone to bring it to pass, whether the recipient believes it or not. As defined earlier, the reason is to fulfill God's purpose or plan for mankind.

An example of such prophecy is that given to Manoah and his wife in Judges 13. An angel was sent to Manaoh's wife, who was barren; she was told she would bear a son who was to be a Nazarite from the womb. This prophecy went further to say that the son to be born would deliver Israel out of the hand of the Philistines. This prophecy about Manoah's unborn miracle child, Samson, eventually was fulfilled in him. Although he lived a reckless life with women and was stubborn, he still delivered the Israelites from the hands of the Philistines, just as God had said. His reckless behavior did not stop God from using Him to perform what he was destined to do. Why? Because he had an attached prophecy; that is why when Samson disobeyed God and allowed a razor to touch his hair; God did not completely forsake him. Instead, God enabled him to repent and allowed his hair to grow back so that the prophecy that went forth before him might be fulfilled. The plan of God to use Samson to kill the Philistines could not be changed.

This type of prophecy was also given to Abraham. The LORD said to him, that he would be a father of many nations. He was told that his children would be like the sand on the seashore and the stars in the sky. Now this was laughable. Abraham did not have any child at the time this word was told to him, and considering the fact that Sarah his wife was past childbearing age and he was now old, this looked totally impossible. But God had chosen Abraham to be the father of the people He wanted a relationship with, and Sarah's condition was not going to stop His sovereign plan and purpose. So, God made His promise manifest even after Abraham went out of God's perfect will and fathered Ishmael. This prophecy of Abraham becoming a father of many nations was attached to Sarah, not Haggai, and as such its fulfillment could only be through Abraham and Sarah.

In non-personal prophecies even when we make mistakes like Samson and Abraham, or we are reluctant to obey His will at first, like Joseph, the husband of Mary, God still forgives and fulfill His original plan. This of course is not a ticket to be disobedient, but to stress the fact that nothing can stop prophetic words from manifesting when it involves God's divine plan and purpose for benefiting all of mankind and not just an individual.

Another example of someone who had an attached prophecy was Paul. God gave Ananias a word about Saul (Paul) when He told him to go and pray for Saul.

And the LORD said unto him, Arise, and go into the street which is called Straight, and enquire in the house of Judas for one called Saul, of Tarsus: for, behold, he prayeth. And he had seen in a vision a man named Ananias coming in, and putting his hand on him, that he might receive his sight. Then Ananias answered, LORD, I have heard by many of this man, how much evil he

hath done to thy saints in Jerusalem. And here
he hath authority from the chief priest to bind
all that call on thy name. But the LORD said
unto him, go thy way: for he is a chosen vessel
unto me to bear my name before thy gentiles
and kings and the children of Israel: for I will
show him how great things he must suffer for
my name's sake.

Acts 9:11-16

This prophecy was spoken about the Apostle Paul, and
it was attached to him. We will agree that Saul was not
the only person that was persecuting God's people in
his time. But he was the only one in scriptures that had
such a dramatic encounter with God. True to the word
of the LORD to Ananias, Paul received great a revelation from God to the gentiles and to the Jews as well.
He also suffered many things for the gospel; he was
beaten, stoned, shipwrecked; yet Paul remained strong.
It is my belief that Paul was able to fulfill all that God
said about him, despite all that he faced, because there
was a prophecy about him that was not dependant on
him for its fulfillment, but totally on God.

The prophecy given to Rebecca is another great
example in this category of prophecies. The Bible tells
us that Isaac and Rebecca could not have children,
because she was barren. Isaac prayed to God to bless
his wife, and she became pregnant. During this pregnancy, Rebecca felt the children struggled in her womb,
and she went to inquire of the LORD. The answer she
received was:

And the LORD said unto her, two nations are in thy womb, and two manner of people shall be separated from thy bowels; and the one shall be stronger than the other people; and the elder shall serve the younger.

Genesis 25:23

It was indeed seen that the younger son became the elder, because Esau sold his birth right to his younger brother, Jacob. The interesting point about this story is that Rebecca favored her younger son, Jacob, over her eldest. Something she probably would not have done had she not received that word from God. So did God make her love one child more than the other? Of course not, but He allowed the existing situation in other to accomplish His purpose for Jacob (who had a personal attached prophecy), who we know later became the father of the nation of Israel.

The examples mentioned thus far are about people. Now let's us look at a non-personal prophecy attached to a place. The place where Jesus was to be born is a great example to consider, and this prophecy had a dramatic fulfillment. I use the word *dramatic* because the environment and situations had to be changed drastically in order for this to come to past. The Bible records that the Prophet Micah prophesied in the book of Micah 5:2, that Jesus will come out of Bethlehem.

But thou, Bethlehem Ephratah, though thou be little among the thousands of Judah, yet out of thee shall he come forth unto me that is to

be ruler in Israel; whose goings forth have been
from of old, from everlasting.

This prophecy refers to the birthplace of Jesus, and it
says that it will be Bethlehem. This word was given a
long time before Jesus was to be born. Imagine this,
Mary was pregnant and was almost giving birth, but she
and Joseph were still in Nazareth in the city of Galilee.
It is a fact that Mary and Joseph believed the prophecies
of God (if they did not believe before, the pregnancy
was enough proof for them to later believe); it can be
said also that they knew all the prophecies concerning
the Messiah (I believe that they did know after they
became directly involved in its manifestation). Then it
is not presumptuous to say that Joseph and Mary must
have thought about how they were still in Nazareth
when the child was to be born in Bethlehem.

They may have thought of going to Bethlehem, but
it was not convenient for them with Mary, who was far
gone in her pregnancy, and Joseph really not having
the money to make the trip, especially in the desert.
This was a hard task to do. You see Joseph and Mary
could not have fulfilled this prophecy by themselves,
just like in all the other examples. God had to super-
naturally allow a situation to happen that would give
Joseph and Mary no choice, but to go to Bethlehem.
So what did God do? He used the emperor of Rome,
Caesar Augustus, to make a decree (Luke 2:1-7) that
everyone should be taxed in his own city. Joseph, being

of the household of David, had to go to Bethlehem of Judea, and this was where Jesus was born. Wow! How so like God to use who, what, and any means to bring His word to pass.

PERSONAL PROPHECIES

Personal prophecies are always attached. They are those that are given specifically to an individual in respect to some aspect of his or her life. This type of prophecy involves the co-operation (participation) of the recipient. That is, God cannot bring it to pass if the one receiving the prophecy does not respond to it, because it is not a non-personal prophecy. Its fulfillment does not determine or change an event that affects humanity. The only thing that it affects is the recipient and what concerns him or her. For this reason its manifestations depends partly on God and on the recipient.

There are several factors that affect the manifestation of personal prophecies. Examples of some are: faith, season, time, patience, speaking or declarations of God's word, and obedience to instructions. Another very interesting factor that has evolved over the years is this misunderstanding called "it did not bear witness with my spirit."

It is imperative that I stress the fact that many true prophets have been termed false, because what they said did not come to pass. It is important to note that 90 percent of the time these factors play the major role why such prophecies are aborted. It entirely was sent down the drain by the recipient of these words who could not adhere to the operation of these factors. The remaining 10 percent of the time is the prophet's error.

Factors that Affect the Manifestations of Personal Prophecies

Faith

The book of Hebrews 11 teaches us about faith. One very important lesson is that it is impossible to please God without it. It goes further to say that for us to come to God, we must believe that He is and that He will reward those who will seek Him diligently (truthfully). The key words here are that *God is*. Some people believe that God was and will be. But the scriptures say that *He is*. This means that God is alive and rules and reigns in the affairs of men. If we understand this truth, then we know that He is a speaking God, and He speaks by whichever means He chooses. Of course the only infallible way by which God speaks is through His Word, the Bible. But He also speaks through people, especially the prophets.

The question then is, do we believe that God has prophets today, and do they hear from God? This is where faith as a factor comes in to play. You see if we do not believe that there are prophets set in the body of Christ in this age, then it is conclusive that we will not believe a prophetic word given by any such person. The stumbling block to receiving God's messages from a prophet, I believe, goes further than what we choose to identify. We have used all kinds of excuses, such as false prophecy, to "it does not bear witness with me," to reject a prophetic word. However, on closer examination the problem really is that we do not believe that God can speak expressly about a particular situation, in a timely manner, and that He can do so through His prophets. Let us examine Amos 3:7 and 2 Chronicles 20:20 respectively.

> Surely the LORD God will do nothing, but He revealeth His secrets unto His servants the prophets.
>
> Amos 3:7

> And they rose up early in the morning, and went forth into the wilderness of Tekoa: and as they went forth, Jehoshaphat stood and said, hear me, O Judah, and ye inhabitants of Jerusalem; Believe in the LORD your God, so shall ye be established; believe His prophets, so shall ye prosper.
>
> 2 Chronicles 20:20

God clearly states in the Bible that He talks to His prophets and tells them things that may not be common knowledge to everybody else. The scripture went further to advise us to believe in God's words through the prophets so that we can prosper. The question is do we believe these scriptures.

All manner of reasons have been given by the church to explain these verses. Some say that these verses are in the Old Testament and as such do not apply any more in the new covenant. Others say that we are all prophets in the New Testament, and, as such, we do not need anyone to tell us "thus said the LORD," because God will speak to us Himself. This fallacy, which has its roots in unbelief, has been propagated for so long that it has become acceptable in the body of Christ. It is a fallacy, because there are prophets in the New Testament (Ephesians 4:11 and 1 Corinthians 12:27-29), and everyone is not called into the same office, as the Apostle Paul explains in 1 Corinthians 12. So, if the prophetic office is still needed in the New Testament as it was in the Old Testament, then the words that God speaks through the prophets are still valid today and will be until Jesus comes again, where there will be no need for the five-fold ministry.

Faith is to believe all of God's word. We are not to pick and choose those that only make sense to us. This is why the Bible says that God uses the foolish things of the world to confound the wise. Who is the wise in this context? It is he that thinks that the word of God should always be rationally explained at all times.

A person with such mindset—even if they are Christians—cannot receive a prophet and, therefore, does not believe any message given by God through this vehicle. This kind of person will not see a manifestation of the word given because he is in unbelief.

Let us consider a practical example. A prophet is sent by God to give a prophecy to a church congregation. The word given is: "God says there is a breakthrough for those who have applied for jobs for a while and have had no responses from anyone. In three days you will be called to that job you applied for." There will be mixed responses to this word given by the prophet by those seeking employment. Some will mock it, others will not believe it, but the ones who will receive it as God's word will see the manifestation. And if none of them received the word, there will not be a manifestation. Does this make the prophet false? No! It means that there was no fertile ground for the word to germinate (like the parable of the sower), and as such it did not bear fruits. Faith is a key ingredient in the manifestations of personal prophecies, and its importance cannot be overemphasized. Faith is what enables us to receive from God that which He has promised or said.

This factor of faith in prophecy manifestations have been completely misunderstood by a lot of people. It is sad to say that many called to frontline ministry also have a wrong perspective of this factor. Some teach that when a prophet gives a word to a person or people, if that word is not inspiring (for example, the word was to pray against sudden death), then the prophet who gave the word did so because he or she did not have faith to believe otherwise. The scripture that they base this on is that we prophesy according to our proportion of faith. They argue that if the prophet had faith he would not have delivered a word that is not inspirational. It is imperative to explain that what the Bible means about prophesying according to our proportion of faith is that if a person with a prophetic word does not believe that what he is about to say is from God, then he should not say it. Let us take a hypothetical example of such a situation for better understanding. God sends a prophetess to a man named John, and this is the word she is to deliver.

> Thus saith the LORD unto you John. There is need for much prayer for your family so that the plan of the enemy to take a life prematurely will not come to pass.

Can God use a prophet to deliver such a word? Of cause He can. Jesus told Simon in Luke 22:31-32 that Satan desired to sift him as wheat, but He prayed for him so that his faith will not fail.

If the prophetess sent to John does not believe that this is God speaking, then she should not go. However, if she is convinced that it is God, then she should deliver the message. Now, there are different ways that one can react to this word. The set of people who have totally misunderstood faith and prophecy say that the prophetess—if she had faith—should never have given the message because God has already given John (being a Christian) victory over the devil, and, as such, he cannot take a life of anyone in his family, and so God cannot send such a word to John. So the prophetess is termed false. While the set that understands the role of faith in a prophetic word knows that God can warn His people about the plan of the adversary. He hears the word and prays in faith against such attack.

In analyzing both sets of Christians, the first set obviously do not know the difference between the gifts of prophecy being manifested from the word of wisdom. You see, the word to John was not a prophecy (hence it was not a word to inspire him) instead it was a word of wisdom (requires him to make a decision to pray or not to pray, just like Jesus prayed for Simon so that Satan's plan to destroy him would be aborted). If John prays, the situation will be averted, and if John does not pray, he will most likely experience death in his family if God does not show mercy.

The role of faith in receiving a prophetic word from God is totally dependant upon the recipient, and it is pivotal to how it all plays out at the end of the day.

Season

The book of Ecclesiastics says that there is a season and a time for every purpose under the heaven. This book written by King Solomon emphasizes the fact that the different circumstances and events that happen in the life of man have their seasons and appointed time, and that God makes everything beautiful in His time (Ecclesiastics 3:1-11).

God has seasons for specific things to come to pass in the lives of His people, although many Christians do not believe or accept this. I have heard people say that as long as you have faith, you can make anything happen immediately. There is a lack of balance in such statement, because the word of God clearly talks about seasons (Ecclesiastics 1). All over the scriptures, it is seen that God has brought things to pass in seasons. In the same manner, God still has seasons for some of His spoken word today.

The lack of understanding of this factor has robbed many believers of the manifestation of prophetic words given by God through His prophets. Most of the time, we expect the prophecy to come to pass immediately or when we think it should. When this does not fall within our expected time, the prophecy is deemed wrong, and the prophet is called false.

It is important to note that if a recipient of a prophetic word stops believing in that prophecy before its season of manifestation, that prophecy can be aborted. In other words, it may never come to pass. This is due to the fact that at this point faith is no longer in operation, which means that God is not compelled to bring it to pass. What God requires us to do is to keep believing the word until its season of manifestation comes.

Let us consider some biblical examples. God told Abraham in Genesis 15 that he was going to have a child. Abraham believed God for many years, but this promise was not made manifest. It did not come to pass for a long time because it was not yet the season for it. The Bible makes this clear in Genesis 18:11-14.

> Now Abraham and Sarah were old and well stricken in age; and it ceased to be with Sarah after the manner of women. Therefore, Sarah laughed within herself, saying, after I am waxed old shall I have pleasure, my LORD being old also? And the LORD said unto Abraham, wherefore did Sarah laugh, saying, shall I of a surety bear a child, which am old? Is any thing too hard for the LORD? At the time appointed I will return unto thee, according to the time, of life and Sarah shall have a son.

The Bible says here that there was an appointed time. That means that there was a season for Sarah to bear her son. Of course, Abraham and Sarah did not know this at the time. In like manner, God still gives his people specific words today whether through prophecy or Bible promises that would be fulfilled in seasons.

There are different seasons for fulfillment for different individuals. There was a season for the LORD Jesus to be born, as there is another set season for His return. Anyone who is conversant with the Bible is aware that if we are not already in the season of the second coming of our LORD Jesus, then we are very close. But we cannot will (faith) Him to come before the appointed time. In the same way, when a prophetic word is spoken to a recipient, and that word has a set season for manifestation, it will not happen until its season is reached.

Many personal prophecies have been aborted, because of this factor. It is important to note that if God sets a season for a prophetic word to come to pass, it is for our own benefit. In this circumstance, our faith cannot will it to come to pass before time. Instead faith in such seemly impossible situations is to continue to believe until its season of manifestation in order for it to be physically seen.

Time

This is another factor that comes into play in personal prophecies. Time not to be confused with appointed time (which means season), is dependent on the recipient of the prophecy; while seasons are totally controlled by God, we have been left with the control of time. By this I mean that we are not to allow time to control us. One major enemy that we have to conquer as Christians is looking at the clock (time). If we allow time to dictate our lives, we will not be able to see the fulfillment of many prophetic words. The time factor will be more understood if we consider some examples.

The book of 1 Samuel 13:5-14 records the story of King Saul offering sacrifice to God, because he could not wait for Samuel to come. Samuel told Saul that he would come in seven days, and, for some reason, he delayed. What did Saul do? He disobeyed God's commandments and offered sacrifice to God himself. Saul's inability to wait for Samuel—his fear of time getting by resulted in his disobedience, which cost him the kingdom.

A similar situation also occurred with Abraham, the father of faith. God promised him a son, but God was too long in manifesting His word so Abraham went into Haggai and had Ishmael (Genesis 15 and 16). Does this ring a bell? How many times have we gone on our own because we think God took to long to perform what He said either through a prophet or in His word that He would do? How many times have we gone and had babies out of wedlock because God's promise of a husband took too long to come to pass and we believed that the proverbial biological clock is ticking? Or how often have we married the wrong people, done a bad business deal, compromised our faith, all because we kept looking at time and were in a rush to get the prophecies we had received fulfilled immediately. We allow the time factor to make the promises of and prophetic words from God look like a lie. God is not controlled by time. We are, if we allow it. If we learn to put this monster called *time* under subjection by overcoming it with the fruit of patience and sometimes long-suffering (patience extended), many personal prophecies will come to pass.

Patience

> And besides this, giving all diligence, add to your faith virtue…and patience and to patience godliness.
>
> 2 Peter 1:5-6

The book of Peter tells us to add several other attributes to our faith, and one of them is *patience*. Wow! This is the factor many people do not want to believe nor discuss. You see, some people believe that as long as you have faith, there should be no waiting period before you see in the physical what you have prayed for. The Bible, however, disagrees with this doctrine. Please do not misunderstand me, of course there are times that immediate manifestations of answered prayers are seen, but most of the time, there is a waiting period which varies according to God's will for that person in that specific situation. I say God's will, because it is God's will for us to grow and mature in Him, and one way of achieving this is by exercising our faith. Thus a waiting period always allows a true Christian to use their faith and, in so doing, grow in the things of God; after all, the Bible says that patience brings forth experience (Romans 5:4). Hence waiting is a necessary part of the Christian journey.

The only way to overcome the unrest of waiting is patience. Patience is a virtue as the saying goes, and a virtue that must be practiced when you receive a prophetic word from God. When a prophecy is given to you, more often than not, your faith in that spoken word will be tried by God and tempted by the devil. That is why in most cases, the very opposite of what was spoken to you in prophecy happens first. The question becomes, do you believe what was said or not, and how much do you believe? A person who believed the word but has not patience will easily loose the word. That is the prophetic word will not come to pass because it tarried, and the person could not wait for it. Habakkuk 2:3 clearly admonishes us to wait for the vision, and if it tarries we should still wait for it because it will surely come to pass.

The greatest fear I believe the believer has, is not witnessing the manifesting of a prophecy after being patient. The very thought of this can rob us of our faith and try to steal the word of God. Reassurance of what you believe is very important at this point. If you did not believe originally that the prophecy was from God (although it was), then the degree of doubt that will creep in will be enormous, for there is nothing to stand on when the doubt tries to creep in. It becomes very easy to say, "I knew that was never going to happen anyway" instead of saying "God has spoken it, that settles it." A person that gets to this point can abort the manifestations of his or her prophecy. The importance of patience in seeing the promises of God fulfilled cannot be overemphasized. Sometimes, patience is not enough; it has to be extended. This is the place where most Christians falter or fail. When the wait becomes long and longer, and the years become close to double digits, even mature prophecy believing, Bible understanding Christians can begin to doubt their faith and what God said. At this point, constantly bringing the prophetic word to remembrance, as well as the fruit of longsuffering (patience extended) is a key factor to having a fulfillment of that prophetic word that was received.

Declarations of God's Word

The book of Romans 4:17 says that God calls those things that are not as though they were. Throughout the book of Genesis during creation, we find that God called everything into being (Genesis 1). The operative word here is *called*. In order to call anything, words have to be spoken. Thus, God spoke everything into creation, making spiritual (invisible) things to become natural and visible. This gives us an example of what can happen through the act of speaking like God. I use the word like God because it is not just in the speaking of anything that creativity comes, but in the act of declaring what God tells us to say, and believing that it is, as was said. The scripture says that we believe, therefore, we speak.

It was and still is God's plan and purpose for us to be speaking beings. God designed it that in order to get His will for us to be made manifest, we have to agree with Him. This agreement in part is demonstrated when we declare what He says. Take for example in the garden of Eden; God brought all the animals before Adam to see what he would call them. The Bible says that whatever Adam called them were their names (Genesis 2:19-20).

Adam was first a spiritual being like God, sinless in nature, but covered in flesh. His spiritual nature was in tune with God, and that is why God could come and fellowship with him in the garden, in the cool of the day. Adam was like God in everything, power and all, except that he had flesh. Adam had so much of

God within him that he was given dominion over the earth. In view of this, it can be said that God's plan for Adam was already downloaded into his spiritual being when he was created. In lieu of this, it can be deduced that whatever Adam called the animals was what God wanted them to be called. Adam, therefore, naming the animals was God's will, being fulfilled through Adam. In like manner, when God speaks to us concerning our future either by prophecy, vision, or dreams, He is bringing to our knowledge that which was already downloaded into us when we were created, but cannot really perceive fully with our natural minds; that which needs to be manifested in our lives having being settled in the spirit realm.

In order for us to experience this we have to declare in agreement with God that it is as He has downloaded into our being from the beginning. Adam had to call the animals that which God had already called them in his spirit. He declared it and, in so doing, agreed with God. In declaring the word, we are fighting a good warfare with the prophecy that we have received as Apostle Paul told Timothy (1Timothy 1:18). The importance of constantly declaring that word cannot be overemphasized. God's system of personal prophecies coming to pass includes confessing (declaring) what you have heard and believed. Unfortunately, we have a way of reasoning when we receive a prophetic word. We think that since God said it, it must come to pass whether we believe it or not. This concept is only true for non-personal prophecies (read the chapter on non-personal prophecies) and certainly wrong for personal prophecies.

The book of Habakkuk 2:2 tells us to write the vision down and to make it plain upon tables, so that he who reads it should run with it. Well what does this mean? This means that the main objective of this commandment is for the vision not to be forgotten. Therefore, the writing down can be taken literally. The recipient should write whatever God tells him (whether by vision, dreams or prophecies) down on paper. In the process of writing it down on paper, it is also written in the tablets of his heart. It is important to note that in writing and reading the word, it allows for remembrance of that word at a later time. The more the word is remembered and declared, the more likely it is not forgotten. The second part of what prophet Habakkuk said is to run with the vision after it is written down. Run to where or to what? Now in this aspect, the prophet did not mean a literal running, but a keeping of that God-given word *alive*. Keeping the word alive in our hearts gives hope. The Bible says, "hope maketh not ashamed" (Romans 5:5). That means that a person who hopes in what God has said will get what God has promised him or her. Why? Because hope makes our perception of the possibility of the word being fulfilled more real. This in turn builds faith, which enables us to wait for that prophecy to be made manifest in its appointed time (season).

For the vision is yet for an appointed time, but at the end it shall speak, and not lie: though it tarry, wait for it; because it will surely come, it will not tarry.

Habakkuk 2:3

Bearing Witness to Prophecies

One of the greatest hindrances to receiving a prophetic word from God by Christians who believe in the prophetic office is, "it does not bear witness with me." This has become a slogan in the Christian world, used to imply that if God is really the one speaking through the prophet, then God would have said it to them first. In other words, the message given ought to be a confirmation of what God already told them. What utter nonsense. There is no place in scriptures where it is said that a prophet or prophetess only speaks to confirm what is already known. On the contrary, almost all the time God used the prophetic office to perform a task the people had no prior knowledge of the task.

The term bearing witness, I believe, stemmed from the fact that the Bible says that the prophetic word has to be judged. God set this in place to eliminate or minimize errors that may arise from those operating in the prophetic office. However, this scripture has been taken totally out of content and used instead to persecute those who are called to this ministry. Let us examine 1 Corinthians 14:29-32.

> Let the prophets speak two or three, and let the other judge. If any thing be revealed to another that sitteth by, let the first hold his peace. For ye may all prophesy one by one, that all may learn, and all may be comforted. And the spirits of the prophets are subject to the prophets.

The Bible says that the prophets are to be the judge of one another not just anyone. Why? They operate in the same office and, as such, will be able to discern a false prophet or prophecy much quicker and more accurately than just anyone. This is due to the anointing that rest on the office. This type of scenario, where a prophet had to judge another prophet, is recorded in the book of Jeremiah. In this case, Hananiah the prophet gave a false word to King Zedekiah that the yoke of King Nebuchadnezzar would be broken off the neck of all nations within the space of two years. Jeremiah challenged that word by correcting it with another prophecy (Jeremiah 28). In an another story, Jeremiah was also sent to correct the prophecy that some prophets gave the same king telling him that he shall not serve the king of Babylon; and the prophets also told the priest that the vessels of the LORD, which were taken to Babylon, would be brought back in a short time (Jeremiah 27:12-16).

There is one important point that is common to these two cited examples. God sent a second prophet to correct the wrong that the first one did. I believe that even now, God still does the same thing. If a prophet gives a word that is a lie to the receiver, one way or another God allows another prophet to correct that wrong. It is my belief that a prophet is more equipped to judge another because of the anointing that rest on the office. The question that arises then is how does the prophet judge one another? This simply means that if there is more than one prophet in a place, they should all feel the prophetic anointing in the atmosphere when it arises irrespective of whom God uses to deliver the word. For example, I went to a prophetic meeting that lasted for five days, and this man of God was not used in prophetic utterances through the meetings. People kept saying, "Oh, what is going on? When will he say something?"

He was having a wonderful teaching session, but the people wanted to hear, "Thus said the LORD" (we must be careful as prophets not to be pressured into self-acting). Anyway, on one of the days, almost at the end of the meeting, the man of God came into the meeting, and I said to my friend sitting next to me, "He is going to prophesy and minister in the prophetic anointing today. She said, "How do you know?" I could not really explain it to her, but I could see and feel the prophetic unction in the atmosphere. I was ready to prophesy myself (if you walk regularly in this office, you will know what I am talking about). And truly, before he got to the middle of his teachings, the prophetic anointing took over, and people were told very specific things, and deliverance was wrought that day. I was in the room that day, and if I was to judge if the man was a true prophet, or if he gave the correct words, I would have to say "yes." Yes, because it was obvious that God was there, and the prophetic anointing was heavy. Any true prophet in that room would have had the same witnessing—that the atmosphere was "prophetically charged."

In another meeting that I was invited to in one of the churches in Maryland, many guest speakers were invited to speak on different days. On one of the days, I walked into the church and said to myself *there is a prophet in this meeting.* How did I know? A prophetic atmosphere hit me as I entered the room. Any true and matured prophet would have felt it. Guess what? The minister for that day was a prophet and God used him powerfully to His glory. The point that I am trying to make with these examples is that a prophet can judge a prophet because they "catch" each other in the spirit. The question might be asked if someone who is not a prophet can judge a prophet. The answer is "yes," but the person has to be a matured, unbiased, scripture-knowing believer. It is much better if that person also have the gift of discernment of spirits.

Another important point that Paul makes in 1 Corinthians 14 is that the prophet should speak one by one. That is when something is revealed to one by God, the others may have the same message (hence let them speak one by one). So if one has it, the others do not have to speak it, except God says so for confirmation purposes. Note that the confirmation to the recipient does not necessarily mean that he or she already heard God for themselves but rather for emphasis. That is, God can allow more than one prophet to give the same message to the same person in order to stress the importance of what was being said. This does not negate the fact that the recipient may have been told the same word by God. God can and does speak to His people without the prophets, especially when the word is personal. But He has also set in place a spiritual antenna that picks up His voice in the spirit much quicker. In the church it is the prophetic office. That is not to say that the other ministerial offices may not perceive or know when God is communicating in this manner with His people. However, the prophetic office is anointed to function specifically in this capacity.

Another scripture I believe some people use to justify, "It did not bear witness with my spirit," is 1 Thessalonians 5:21, "Prove all things; hold fast that which is good."

Let us not forget that the presiding verse says, "Despise not prophesying." If we study people who always say, "It does not bear witness with me," we will find out that they have some kind of problem with prophecies. Either they do not believe in it, or they refuse to accept the person through whom the prophecy is given. Whichever way, it is an example of despising prophecies. Most of the people who despise prophecies blame it on proving all things. It is the truth that God says we are to prove all things. But the question is how are we supposed to accomplish this? The answer is in 1 John 4:1-3.

> Beloved, believe not every spirit, but try the spirits whether they are of God: because many false prophets are gone out into the world. Hereby know ye the Spirit of God: Every spirit that confesseth that Jesus Christ is come in the flesh is of God: And every spirit that confesseth not that Jesus Christ is come in the flesh is not of God: and this is that spirit of antichrist, whereof ye have heard that it should come; and even now already is it in the world.

How do you know God's spirit? If it confesses that Jesus Christ is LORD. In other words, the judging that God is talking about (1 Corinthians 14:29) as well as proving all things refers to us making sure that whatever we listen to, whether it is preaching, teaching, or a word of prophecy, it should be in line with the word of God. In other words, a prophet who tells you to steal, kill, lie, commit adultery, fornicate, or break any other laws of God is a false prophet. That word should not bear witness with your spirit, because it is contrary to scripture. This means that you as a believer have to study God's word otherwise you will not know which word of prophecy given to you is contrary to the word of God. So when God said, "prove all things," it means compare all things with the word of God. Therefore, if a prophetic word is given to you, and it is contrary to scripture, you should not receive it. However, if that word is not contrary to scripture, there is nothing to prove, therefore, it does not have to bear witness with you. That it does not bear witness with you does not make the word false. It just means that your "spiritual antenna" did or could not pick up the word in the spirit realm.

This is where the prophets judging one another can be seen. You see, if the word given is not against scripture, and it still does not bear witness with the recipient, the only way to know if the word is from God (and not just the recipient having a problem with it, because it does not stroke his or her ego), is for another prophet who operates under the same anointing to judge it. Just like in the case of Jeremiah and Hananiah. The false word given was not against any written commandments of God. In fact the words were favorable to the king, yet it was not from God. If the prophetic words were to be judged by the church in this day, it is my belief that 99 percent will judge Jeremiah wrong and Hananiah to be right. This is what is happening in the body of Christ today. If the word is not full of goodies, we say that it does not bear witness with us. How unfortunate, for we have missed God's warnings and even blessings by persecuting the prophet, and then we go astray and wonder why God did not warn us. It is time that we disallow this monster of "it does not bear witness with my spirit," to stop placing a barricade in our minds. Let us look at some reasons why the prophetic word may not bear witness with you.

There are several reasons why a person may not have prior knowledge of a word spoken to him or her by a prophet. One of which is God did not tell you. God sent the prophet Samuel to go to Saul and anoint him as king in 1 Samuel 9:27, 10:1, and 15:1 as well as to anoint David as king in 1 Samuel 16:1, 11-13. In both of these instances, neither Saul nor David knew before that day that they were to be king over Israel. Did that make Samuel a liar or a false prophet for anointing them as king? No. Though David was usually led by God, as we can see in his killing of the bear and the lion (1 Samuel 17:34 - 36), in killing the Philistines giant Goliath, (1 Samuel 17:48-51) and in his playing the harp for Saul (1 Samuel 16:14-23). He still did not know he was to be king of Israel until the day Samuel anointed him. But wait a minute, I thought David both knew and served God. Why then did God not communicate with him about being king directly? Because God is who He is, He does what he wants and how He chooses to do it is His decision alone. That is why He is God. One can argue that David was in the Old Testament and as such did not have the spirit of God residing within him; therefore, he was not programmed to hear God for himself. Although David was not filled with the Holy Ghost, we will all agree that he knew how to hear from God. Or how else can we explain all of his messianic Psalms.

Hearing from God for himself was not David's problem. God chose to send a prophet to him about making him king, because that was how God planned it. The interesting fact is that today He still chooses sometimes to send a prophet to give a word or perform a specific task. God even sends one prophet to another prophet. You may ask the question, does the prophet who is given the word already know the word? The answer is, not all the time. Just like for anybody else, sometimes the prophet receives a word, and it will be totally new to him. A prophetic word will not always bear witness with your spirit. The only witness it needs to bear is that it in line with the word of God as explained earlier. David believed the word of God that he would become king. He believed it though; it was greatly tried, and it looked like it will not happen (with Saul's attempt to kill him and everything else that hindered him), David knew that he would be king, and it was fulfilled.

Let us look at three practical examples of how people can respond to the same prophetic word where they had no prior knowledge of it.

A prophet gives a word to a couple that they will have a child. This couple has stopped bearing children. The wife has tied her tubes because they do not want any more children, so it is easy for this couple to perceive the word to be incorrect. One reason this couple perceives the word to be incorrect is that, if the prophet is real, he would have known about the tied tubes, therefore, they conclude that the prophecy cannot be from God. Another reason why this word can be perceived as false is that this couple does not want God to override their plans of not having more children. Thus, disbelieving the word is more believable.

In another example this couple that has one child wanted another, but is now past childbearing age. Then a prophet gives them a word that God will give them another child. It is also easy for this couple to perceive that the word is wrong because science says it cannot happen anymore. So the real issue here is that this couple do not see beyond the natural to the supernatural provision of God, so they are done with child bearing and as such do not receive the prophecy.

In the third example, this couple wants children. They have been praying for it since they were young and now are getting older. But there is yet no manifestation. This couple does not give up hope for their children but continues to believe God. Then a prophet comes and gives them a word that they will have children. This couple is likely to receive the word because they have been in expectation of this miracle. In this instance, the prophet is perceived as true.

Looking at these three examples, you come to see what really plays out in the minds of people who are given a prophetic word. The different mindset influences the decision to accept or not to accept it. You see, the prophet was not known by any of the people whom he was sent to. He was sent to three different homes with different situations, but with the same message from God. The response was only positive in one situ-

BEARING WITNESS TO PROPHECIES

ation. So what made the couple in the third example receive the word?

The first conclusion 90 percent of people will jump to is that the word was received because it bore witness with the couple who wanted children. Now that is true, it did bear witness with them; however, that the other two did not believe it does not make the word wrong. Let us analyze these examples further; in the first example, the couple had finished having children, they were not on a break from child bearing, they were completely done. But God was not finished with them yet. And so God was sending them a word to prepare them for what was ahead, so that when they felt the urge to untie the wife's tubes, they would know it was God's plan. The child to be brought forth might be the one God wanted to use for a specific task.

The same thing applies to the couple in the second example. Although they were past childbearing age, God might have wanted to show His supremacy over all things for His glory. And so He decided to use them in His plan. You know just like Abraham in the Bible, God wanted to give them a testimony that will blow the minds of everybody by giving them a child when medically it was impossible. But instead of admitting to lack of faith for this word, it was believed to be wrong. All God required from these couples was for them to say, "though right now I do not see the possibility of this word coming to pass, nor do I understand it, God, if this is You, may Your will be done." Total submission to God's will, even when we do not like, understand, or see it, propels us to the next level of faith. It allows God to open our eyes to see the plan and purpose of the given prophecy more clearly.

Am I saying that the word of prophecy should never bear witness with you? Absolutely not! There are times when it does, especially if you are a person who stays in the presence of God, who has committed himself or herself to praying, fasting, and studying the word of God. One who has learned to discern the voice of God will hear God speak to them. For example, when God gave the word of rebuke and judgment to the prophet Samuel for Eli, Eli already knew what the sin was (1 Samuel 3:11-13). So Samuel's prophetic word from God was not new but rather a confirmation. But God does not always work in this manner. Sometimes, a word from a prophet comes the first time to the recipient that is hearing it.

The point here is that it should not be a doctrine that one will always know what God sends a prophet to say before it is said. A faithful believer can and should hear God for himself or herself, but a prophet can hear God for others, as well as for himself. This is one of the things that make a prophet, a prophet. Otherwise, the prophetic calling is no longer a calling, neither are the gifts associated with the office, a gift. You see, the word of prophecy is a gift, the office of a prophet is a calling, and as such there is an anointing that operates in some particular people that have this calling and gifts which gives them the ability to hear and discern more easily, quickly, and accurately than those who are not called to this office. That being the case, sometimes God can and does give a word to a prophet for someone who has no prior knowledge of it. If the person can receive it, it comes to pass.

If a prophet delivers a message to a person without him having prior knowledge of it, it behooves the recipient to ask God for confirmation of that word if he has a problem with it, rather than discarding or disregarding it. God will send confirmation the best way for that person to receive it, if the person sincerely wants to be obedient to God. And if the prophet made a mistake, God will make that known too. This is how "bearing witness" with us needs to be handled appropriately.

ASSIGNMENTS OF THE PROPHETIC OFFICE

Another important fact about the prophetic office is that God usually gives a prophet an assignment or mandate. What this simply means is the level of work that God has called that prophet to. Usually, the greatness of the work determines the level of the anointing that the person has or will have in the prophetic office. The assignment or mandate differs from one prophet to another, so the greatness of the mantle also differs from one prophet to another.

That a prophet or prophetess has a greater mantle does not make him or her more superior or spiritual than those with lesser mantles. It just means that they have more work to do, so they may become more known or recognized in the society. Sometimes, God calls a prophet to a local assembly, city, state, or nation while He may call others to kings, presidents, or different nations. It is important to note, that the same gifts are at work in all of these mandates, but in different levels of operation.

The prophet that is called to a local assembly will usually receive a word from God for that place. It does not mean that he may not at times hear a word for other people, but it may not be frequent. On the other hand, the prophet that is called to a nation will hear God's instruction(s) for that nation. The same is true for one called to kings. Usually, prophets with great mantles can and do hear God for all manner of peoples and their assignments can be intertwined. That is God can be speaking to them about a local assembly, and at the same time about nations.

It should not be misunderstood that a prophet who is called to a local assembly or to just a city cannot have a great mantle. It is not the number of people that they are called to that makes a mantle great, rather it is the scope of work that they are responsible for. Let me explain further with an example; the prophet Moses had a single assignment. He was to lead the children of Israel out of Egypt to the land God promised them. This assignment can be seen as a calling to a local assembly (because it was the same people). Yet Moses had a great prophetic mantle, because the work was great. The Pentateuch records how difficult a task this was to accomplish. From the different battles fought, to the rebellion of the people he was leading. Moses definitely needed a lot of anointing to be successful.

In the same way, a prophet who is called to a local church may have a lot of work in that place to accomplish. The congregation may be totally rebellious, the pastors may be ignoring God's will and doing their own things, the church may need a prophet who will be in intercession constantly for the great vision of that church, or for the need of that church as the case may be. The point is that a local assembly can have a prophet with a great mantle, because his assignment for that assembly is enormous.

Usually when a prophet or prophetess is called to nations and kings, they are likely to have great mantles and hence great anointing. The reason for this is that much spiritual authority is required on the part of the prophet in other for a king or president, especially one that does not know God, to listen to a spokesman from God, especially one that is not from their nation. It is not every prophet that is called to nations or kings that physically go to these nations and kings throughout their ministry. Most of these assignments can and are done in the spiritual realm. This is why sometimes more than one major assignment at the same time can be given to a prophet called to nations.

One might wonder how these assignments can be fulfilled in the spiritual realm. Remember that a prophet's first responsibility is that of intercession. Therefore, a prophet that God has spoken to about a lot of things has the responsibility of praying concerning what they have been shown. Let us consider an example where God has shown a prophet that a nation is disobedient and needed repentance or calamity was inevitable. It may not be feasible for the prophet to go to that nation, or God may even instruct him not to go physically. In this case, the only way to approach the matter is through intercession. Prayer and fasting is needed until a break through is sensed, or God says that it is okay to stop interceding. Otherwise, prayer continues until the physical evidence of the intercession is seen. This prophet, therefore, has to be conversant with the economic and political happenings of the state, nation, or country that they have adopted in prayer. You may ask, what exactly does the prophet pray for in this situation. The prayer point should be for the nation to come to repentance and for God to send them His word through what ever means that will be effective to accomplish this task. The prophet while praying should prophecy repentance to the people of the nation; he should speak to them as if he was physically in the nation, and of course be sensitive to the leading of the Holy Ghost. A prayer of this fashion will take care of the assignment in the spirit realm.

The book of Daniel 9 is a good biblical example of prophetic prayer. Daniel did not have to go and give a verbal word as in a prophecy.

> In the first year of his reign I Daniel understood by books the number of the years, whereof the word of the LORD came to Jeremiah the prophet, that he would accomplish seventy years in the desolation of Jerusalem. And I set my face unto the LORD, God to seek

by prayer supplications, with fasting, and sackcloth, and ashes: And I prayed unto the LORD
my God, and made my confession, and said,
O LORD, the great and dreadful God, keeping
the covenant and mercy to them that love him,
and to them that keep His commandment; We
have sinned, and have committed iniquity, and
have done wickedly, and have rebelled, even by
departing from thy precepts and from thy judgment: Neither have we hearkened unto thy servants the prophets, which spake in thy name to
our kings, our princes, and our fathers, and to
all the people of the land.

                                            Daniel 9:2-6

As Daniel read the book of the prophet Jeremiah, God
spoke (by revelation) to him about what He told Jeremiah would happen to His people (Jeremiah 25:11-13;
29:10-14). He reminded Daniel about Israel's captivity,
and also about their promised restoration after seventy
years. How did Daniel handle this word (revelation)
from God? He began to pray. The Bible says as soon
as he finished reading the book, he began to intercede
for God's promise of restoration to come to pass. You
might ask? How do I know what he was praying about?
Well, he could not have been praying for their captivity not to occur because Israel was already in captivity. Furthermore, the other verses of Daniel 9 confirm
the prayer point. This prayer point was also confirmed
by the words of God through the angel Gabriel sent
to Daniel to give him instructions about what he had

read in Jeremiah, especially concerning the different time frames for the restoration of Israel, the coming of the Messiah, and much more.

There was no need for Daniel to go and tell the king the revelation he received. He did not try to deliver it as a prophetic word to confirm what was already prophesied earlier, which is what some prophets might do; instead his assignment was taken care of it on his knees. Daniel understood that God wanted him to deal with this by prophetic prayer. Right there in his room, he handled the business in the spirit realm. Daniel had a great work to do as a prophet, even when it did not involve "thus saith the LORD." The revelations that God gave Daniel are still being fulfilled, more so now that we are in the last days. The lessons to be learnt here is that the volume of the work determines the greatness of the mantle and direction is always needed from the Holy Spirit on how to handle a word from God. It behooves the prophet; therefore, to know that it is not all the time that what God is showing or speaking to him involves declaration as in "thus saith the LORD." Rather, what is sometimes required is intercession, teaching, preaching, or even counseling.

In the Bible, there are many prophets. Most of them are from the Old Testament, and some are in the New. But each had something in common. They all had assignments to do. From the major prophets to the minor ones, even to those who were not grouped under these headings. There were no exemptions. A prophet is always on duty, waiting to hear God's heart for the people and following through when he hears from God either in prayer, declarations, or both. It is important to note that assignments can be the same through out the ministry of a prophet, or it can change from season to season. It becomes the responsibility of the prophet to know what his or her assignment is, or when one is over, and a new one begins. It is imperative that a prophet handles every assignment in total obedience to God's instruction, no matter if it is a major or minor work.

You might ask, "What if I am not called to be a great prophet or prophetess?" or "If I am, I never get to be known because I never had conferences, never healed the sick, never received a word from God for kings and presidents. Does that mean that I did not have an assignment?" No, of course not, you did or do have an assignment. The word assignment does not mean a huge job. It is that which God holds you responsible for, and it can be as simple as diligently praying for your pastor or prophesying now and then. However, there are prophets who may not fulfill their assignments because they overlooked it or did not understand it. This predicament usually occurs when the prophet is trying to fulfill self-gain instead of "God-gain," therefore, they do not take the time to wait on God and be clear on what they are to do. They rush in their impatience and make mistakes.

Let us look at an example of a prophet who misunderstood his assignment. While God was giving instructions on what to do about the vision he (the prophet) received for a friend to intercede for him, the prophet instead wanted to give the word he is supposed to pray concerning. This is disobedience, and such attitude can result in the prophet missing his assignments. Prophets who continue in this manner will abort what God has prepared for them and eventually will invoke the wrath of God. Let us study another scenario; in this second example, the prophetess is told to go and give a word to someone about her disobedience to God's instruction. But she refuses to go or tries to make excuses for not going because she is afraid of what the recipient might say. This prophetess has overlooked the assignment. This too is disobedience on the part of the prophetess, and, if she continues like this, she will have the same fate as that in the first example. Please note that invoking the wrath of God does not mean that God will kill them, although that's possible. However, it means that God will hold them accountable for their disobedience in whatever way He sees fit, one of which may include a decrease in the functioning of their prophetic gifts, because of lack of appropriate use. This is where a prophet may begin to start to err—because he ministers in his flesh—if he or she is not careful and is one of the main reasons why training in the prophetic ministry is necessary for all called to this office.

Old Testament Prophets

There are many prophets and prophetesses in the Bible. Some of which we know how they were called by God, and of the others, nothing was mentioned in the scriptures about there calling or mandate. Some had dramatic callings while others were quite simple. Some had great mantles while others did not. Some of these prophets's ministry was before the exile to Babylon (pre-exilic prophets), during the exile (exilic prophets) and after the exile (post- exilic prophets). Then there was a span of about 400 years where there was no prophetic ministry after which came the ministry of the New Testament prophets. No matter the era in which these prophets operated, one thing, however, was common to all of them; they were obedient to God in their areas of assignment no matter how reluctant they felt at firs, how difficult and scary the task was, or the degree of opposition they faced. The next two chapters' focus is on the assignments of prophets in scripture and their obedience to the call. It also points out lessons that can be learned by someone who is called to the prophetic office. Furthermore, it emphasizes the messages (prophetic words) that these prophets were entrusted with; while in other cases, their attitude, strengths or weaknesses are discussed. I pray that as you, the prophet or prophetess, reads this chapter, it will birth in you wisdom and boldness to walk in your calling in Jesus name, amen.

Pre-Exilic Prophets to Israel

The Prophet Jonah

Jonah a pre-exilic prophet had his ministry in Israel during the rule of King Jeroboam, the second, from 793-753 BC. The book of Jonah is an interesting book because it tells a story of how the prophet thinks sometimes when God sends him or her to deliver a message. It shows how we may not always be obedient or willing to go at first. The book also portrays some very dramatic intervention of God as well as His forgiveness. Although the prophetic word was to the Assyrians, it was also for the people of Israel because it made them aware that God loves all manner of people.

The LORD sent Jonah to Nineveh to tell them that God has had enough of their wickedness (Jonah 1:1). But Jonah instead of going to Nineveh went far away from the city and far away from God or so he thought. The question though is, why did Jonah not want to fulfill this assignment? Because he was thinking as many prophets sometimes do when God sends them on some missions; Jonah did not want to go and give a word of destruction, and the people repents, God forgives them, and then, that which he prophesied does not come to pass. Jonah knew that God is merciful, but he felt that the people deserved to be destroyed because of their wickedness. The Assyrians were powerful at that time, and were greatly feared for their cruel acts. Therefore, whatever judgment the people of Nineveh received, they had it coming. Why then should he "rock the boat" by giving them a warning that may cause them to change their way and be spared from destruction. Jonah did not want to go to Nineveh.

If you are a prophet, Jonah's reasoning probably resonates within your hearts. You know that time God sent you as a prophet to go and give a message to a pastor whom you know has been indulging in some hidden sin. That person whom you feel it is time that God exposes the sin and totally destroys him or her. In fact, you have been praying for God's judgment, and now God sends you to go and tell them that you know of that sin. The sin that the pastor is sure no one else is aware of, so the only way you could have known is that God revealed it to you the prophet? Of course if the prophet is not careful, his first response will be not to deliver such a message, for the same reason as Jonah— he wants judgment.

Jonah like us sometimes was disobedient, and he ran away from God. Have you as a prophet ran away from your assignment, because of persecution, hardship, selfish reasons, or any other reason? Do not be like Jonah. God does not take His work lightly. Jonah, because of his rebellion, was thrown inside the belly of the whale (Jonah 1:3-17). The Bible says he was there three days and night. Wow! No person wants the wrath of God upon him, even the least of all the prophets. As God's mouthpiece, we cannot take our assignment lightly or playfully. God requires dedication, commitment, and obedience at all times. If God has called you to the prophetic office, or you are a prophet in training, it is imperative that we learn huge lessons from the book of Jonah. When we are disobedient to God's instructions we receive the consequences of our actions.

When God sends a prophet to a place, it is because God needs a work to be done quickly; decisions need to be made, actions to be taken, and even lives can be at stake if the prophet disobeys his instructions and neglects his assignment. So in such a case of disobedience, God has to take the prophet (person) through a situation as a warning not to do that again as well as a lesson to others. Such was that of Jonah. He found himself in a place where he had to call upon God out of desperation, a place where he came to know God only as the master planner, and that only His will matters. Most of all, Jonah was thought a lesson that there was no place to hide or run away from God. When Jonah came to this knowledge, he prayed to God in the belly of the fish. As prophets, when we realize our mistakes in disobeying a direct order, we repent like Jonah, and God gives us a second chance to carry out the assignment or other assignments.

> And the word of the LORD came unto Jonah the second time, saying, Arise, go unto Nineveh, that great city, and preach unto it the preaching that I bid thee.
>
> Jonah 3:1-2

The sad thing though is that Jonah still did not learn his lesson. After he went and preached (prophesied) in Nineveh, the people repented, and God spared the city. But Jonah was angry (Jonah 3:3-10; 4:1-3) because the people were not destroyed.

It is important to note that in Jonah's preaching; he did not tell the people of Nineveh that God asked them to repent, but instead he told them that God would destroy them for their sins. It was the king of Nineveh who decided to call the nation to repentance himself. So it is probable that Jonah was hoping that the people would not repent, so that God would still destroy the land; hence his anger when they repented and were spared. He wasted his time in going to Nineveh and now, he may be perceived as a false prophet as well, because what he said did not come to pass.

As prophets, when God gives us an assignment, especially when we have a second chance to right that which we did wrong, we must not let our personal image be a hindrance to what God has given to us to accomplish. We must not let what we, the world or the church, thinks dictate our obedience to God. We should not be concerned with "what if the word God is asking me to speak never happens." As long as you are sure that it is God speaking through you, declare the word, and the rest is left for God to perform. Even when the word tarries or does not come to pass, if you are a true prophet, you should not be ashamed or allow people to make you loose confidence in your calling; because we know that there are situations, like in the case of Jonah where the recipient's action determines the outcome of the word given. Therefore, being labeled false should never deter any true prophet from performing his assignment.

The lifestyle of the Prophet Jonah is used as an example to educate the prophet of conflicts that can occur in our minds, while trying to obey an assignment. That is why Jonah's reaction to the word from God was concentrated on more in this passage than the actual message that was delivered to Nineveh.

The Prophetess Deborah

The Prophetess Deborah was a mighty woman of God. She is an example that God can and does use woman to accomplish great things in the body of Christ, and in the world at large. Deborah was the wife of Lapidoth, a judge in Israel and a prophetess of God. All respected her in Israel, and her gender did not interfere with her God-given assignment. Her assignment as a prophetess was to judge Israel in the laws of God and to give prophetic instructions and directions to the whole Nation even in the time of war.

> And she sent and called for Barak the son of Abinoam out of Kedeshnaphtali, and said unto him, hath not the LORD God of Israel commanded, saying, go and draw toward mount Tabor, and take with thee ten thousand men of the children of Naphtali and of the children of Zebulun. And I will draw unto thee to the river Kishon Sisera, the captain of Jabin's army, with his chariots and his multitude; and I will deliver him into thine hand.
>
> Judges 4:6-7

These words the prophetess gave to an army commander, Barak. She literary sent the people to war on God's instructions. What boldness, what great mantle, what an assignment. What word has God put in your mouth as one called to the prophetic office to speak to a president or king or one in great authority? Is it about a war, or peace in a nation, or a people? Do you have to go to that nation or to that person in high authority to deliver the word? How do you approach it or deal with it in this modern day office as a prophet? This is how to handle it. The prophet or prophetess has the responsibility to pray and intercede for that word that is given for it to be delivered. If the recipient of the word can be reached, then approach the person and give the word; if not, pray for God to send them someone who can approach them to deliver the same word given to you. Either way, you have obeyed God and the assignment is fulfilled.

In the case of Deborah, it was easy for her to send for Barak. She was the ruler in Israel at the time, so Barak had to answer her. But Barak's obedience goes beyond his respect for the position of Deborah as a judge or ruler. It went further to her anointing or calling as a prophetess, as one that hears from God. That is why he refused to go to war except Deborah went with them. It is obvious that it is not Deborah's position as a judge that made Barak request her presence at war since there was nothing to judge when they are fighting, instead it was because of her position as a prophetess. Barak knew that God's manifest presence would be there with them if one that was anointed by Him was present in the camp.

> And Barak said unto her, if thou wilt go with me, then I will go: but if thou wilt not go with me, then I will not go.
>
> Judges 4:8

A lesson can be learned from this, Barak saw and understood the office in which Deborah operated. He saw past her disposition as a woman, a wife, and probably a mother. Instead he saw God speaking through Deborah and giving orders. This is what he embraced, and he and the nation's deliverance came in them winning the war. In like manner, when we as a body (the church) see past or beyond the person to understand the office of a prophet in which he/she stands; we too will embrace whatever word God brings through His vessel, and our deliverance also will spring forth. For a word from God, spoken prophetically or read from the scriptures; as long as we believe, it can and does change our lives.

The Prophet Samuel

The Prophet Samuel is an example of a miracle child. His mother, Hannah, could not have children, and so she asked him of the LORD, which is the meaning of the name Samuel. When Samuel was a child, he was brought to the temple and given to God. This began the life of Samuel as a priest and prophet in training until the time of maturity enough to handle his assignment.

Samuel's assignment was many fold. He served as priest, prophet, and judge to Israel. The life of Samuel tells us that a prophet can be multi-talented or multi-faceted in the things of God. That is, God can and does use a prophet to accomplish a whole lot of different things as He sees fit in the body of Christ, and even in the world at large. For Samuel, however, his first major assignment was to deliver a prophetic word to Eli, the priest, his mentor; and what a prophetic word it was. It was one of the most difficult any prophet in training could face or wish they did not have to give. Samuel was to give a word of rebuke and judgment to his mentor (this is an example to those who think that a person who began ministry later than them, cannot be used by God to speak, to those who have been in ministry longer).

> And the LORD said to Samuel, Behold, I will do a thing in Israel, at which both the ears of everyone that heareth it shall tingle. In that day I will perform against Eli all things that I have spoken concerning his house: when I begin, I will also make an end. For I have told him that I will judge his house for ever for the iniquity which he knoweth; because his sons made themselves vile, and he restrained them not. And, therefore, I have sworn unto the house of Eli, that the iniquity of Eli's house shall not be purged with sacrifice nor offering for ever.
>
> 1 Samuel 3:11-14

Wow! Talk about a bearer of bad news. Here is Samuel, a young boy who never heard God speak directly to him before. In fact, the word of the LORD was scarce (precious) in those days, the Bible records that there was no open vision (1 Samuel 3:1). Samuel probably did not even know before he heard the voice of God that he was called to be a prophet. And here is God giving him a prophetic word. What does he do with it? He was still trying to believe that it was God speaking to him, and the word to be delivered was one of rebuke? It will take a very bold, obedient, and mature prophet to deliver such a word to an established man of God not to talk of a prophet in training. But Samuel's training days were over, and his assignment had begun.

Just like Samuel, every true prophet has a training season and a time when their assignment begins. We just have to be in tune with God to be able to know the different times in our lives. All of the time, God will make it known to a prophet one way or another, when assignments begins and training comes to an end, as long as that person is only motivated by God's purpose for their lives and not after personal agenda.

So Samuel graduated from trainee to prophet and delivered the word to Eli. Surprisingly, Eli received the word. I pray that the church today, especially those called to ministry, will take lessons from Eli when God sends His word through a prophet to them. That the people will be humble enough to receive it, or ask God to speak again if they do not understand it, instead of persecuting the messenger. You might say that Eli received the word because God already told it to him (1 Samuel 3:13). That may be true. But I also believe that Eli did not just receive the word only, for God had already spoken to him concerning the matter; but also that he knew Samuel was being raised as a prophet, and he respected that office and feared God. Eli did not have to admit to Samuel that he believed what God had said to him even when he knew that it was true, but he did.

> And Samuel told him everything whit, and hid nothing from him. And he said, it is the LORD: let him do what seemeth him good.
>
> 1 Samuel 3:18

The prophet is to deliver the word of God to all men including mentors, pastors, apostles, teachers, evangelists, or even prophets. However, wisdom is needed to deliver the word with humility and the fear of God.

Samuel, the young boy, grew up to be a great prophet as well as a judge in Israel. Of all the assignments that God used Samuel to perform, one of the most important—I believe—was that of anointing the first king. There are many lessons to be drawn from this aspect in his ministry, but we will look at two of them. One is that God can use a prophet or the gift of prophecy to tell others what their calling is in the body of Christ (example if one is called to the five-fold or other ministries in the church), or a person's gifts or talent in the circular world (called to business, politics). When the people of Israel demanded a monarchial system instead of theocracy, God sent Samuel to anoint Saul as king (1 Samuel 9:17, 10:1). Throughout the Old Testament, prophets anointed all the kings. In like manner today, God still reveals to some prophets (depending on their mantles) the destiny of some people and/or God's purpose for their lives. The Apostle Paul told Timothy in 1 Timothy 4:14 not to neglect the gift that was in him, which was given by prophecy and by the laying on of hands. So Timothy was made aware of his gifts by prophecy, and the laying on of hands activated the gift. Such instructions by God through the prophet to these recipients can be confirmations of what they already know, or it could be new to them.

The second lesson to be learned is that a prophet should never feel rejected when he delivers a word from God, and the recipient rejects it because the person is rejecting God and not the prophet. In the first book of Samuel, the people rejected God and wanted a king, and Samuel felt bad about this. Why did Samuel feel bad? He felt rejected. What the people were really saying was "we do not want Samuel to speak to us anymore." This line of reasoning can be deduced from the fact that God told Samuel that it was Him that was rejected not Samuel (1 Samuel 8:1-7). This buttresses the line of reasoning that Samuel did feel rejection, or God would not have comforted him with the statement about rejection. So the next time God gives you (the prophet) a word to deliver to someone, especially one who should know better and you are rejected, do not feel bad; you are only the messenger and not the originator of the word you delivered. This should give every prophet solace.

The Prophet Amos

Amos was another prophet who was rejected, in this circumstance, not by the people as in the case of Samuel, but by the priest.

> Then Amaziah the priest of Bethel sent to Jeroboam the king of Israel, saying, Amos hath conspired against thee in the mist of the house of Israel: the land is not able to bear all of his words. For thus Amos saith, Jeroboam shall die

> by the sword, and Israel shall surely be led away
> captive out of their own land. Also Amaziah
> said unto Amos, O thou seer, go, flee thee away
> into the land of Judah, and there eat bread, and
> prophesy there: but prophesy not again any
> more at Bethel: for it is the king's chapel, and it
> is the king's court.
>
> Amos 7:10-13

In the prophetic office, there maybe a time when God
sends a prophet with a word to someone or place,
where the response to that word by the person (even
ministers) is not to ever give him a word again. In such
a situation, the prophet is to obey God. As long as he
knows that God is indeed speaking to him. That is
why Amos had this response to Amaziah, the priest.

> Then answered Amos, and said to Amaziah, I
> was no prophet, neither was I a prophet's son;
> but I was an herdman, and a gatherer of syco-
> more fruit: and the LORD took me as I followed
> the flock, and the LORD said unto me, Go,
> prophesy unto my people Israel. Now therefore
> hear thou the word of the LORD: Thou sayest,
> prophesy not against Israel, and drop not thy
> word against the house of Isaac. Therefore thus
> said the LORD; thy wife shall be an harlot in the
> city, and thy sons and thy daughters shall fall by
> the sword, and thy land shall be divided by line;
> and thou shall die in a polluted land: and Israel
> shall surely go into captivity forth of his land.
>
> Amos 7:14-17

In other words, Amos was not stopped by what the priest said. He still gave God's words to the people. Amaziah found out that in fighting Amos, he was actually fighting God and that there are consequences to this action.

Amos served as prophet between 760-750 BC during the reign of King Jeroboam II of Israel and King Uzziah of Judah. He was a contemporary to Jonah and Hosea. His main audience was Israel the northern kingdom, although he lived in Judah the southern kingdom. Amos is an example that God can use or call anyone to be a prophet. By this I mean that one does not have to be from the lineage of prophets, or pastors as is common today. Amos was neither a prophet's son nor a learned man, but God sent him to His people. You do not have to have an education, or come from a family of ministers for God to call you to the prophetic office and give you an assignment.

God sent Amos to Israel with a message of judgment on all the nations that were troubling them at that time (Amos 1and 2) and also with a message of repentance to Israel. Israel was enjoying peace and economic strength at this time, and they became complacent about God. They served other gods and were selfish and materialistic. Furthermore, the rich ignored the needs of the less fortunate and began to oppress the poor amongst them. Amos assignment was to speak against these things (Amos 4 and 5) and call the people back to seek God.

> For thus said the LORD unto the house of Israel, seek ye Me, and ye shall live: But seek not Bethel, nor enter into Gilgal, and pass not into Beer-sheba: for Gilgal shall surely go into captivity, and Bethel shall come to nought. Seek the LORD, and ye shall live; lest he breaks out like fire in the house of Joseph, and devour it, and there be none to quench it in Bethel. Ye who turn judgment to wormwood, and leave off righteousness in the earth, seek him that maketh the seven stars and Orion, and turneth the shadow of death into the morning, and maketh the day dark with night: that calleth for the waters of the sea, and poureth them out upon the face of the earth: The LORD is His name.
>
> Amos 5:4-8

God uses a different style in Amos prophecies. The people are urged to seek God, not by threatening them, but by reminding them of God's power and strength in creation. It is a subtle way of bringing the people back to God. Sometimes, God uses this format to call His people back to repentance today. So a prophet's message of repentance does not always have to be one of "come back to God or die," but can be "come back to God, because God has always been there for you." The method, however, by which the message should or must be delivered is as led of the Holy Ghost.

The ministry of Amos was also one with visions. God spoke to Amos a lot through this means (Amos 7 and 8). In the prophetic office, God sometimes speaks to a prophet by visions, dreams, inner intuition, audibly, or through scriptures. All of these means of hearing from God are still happening today in the life of a believer, and especially in that of a prophet.

The Prophet Hosea

The prophet Hosea functioned in his ministry between 753-715 BC. This places his ministry around the same time with that of Amos, Isaiah and Micah. Hosea's prophetic assignment was to turn the Israelites away from their sin to God; not just by declaring God's words, but also by living a life that exemplifies God's ability and determination to love His people, no matter how wayward they have become. Hosea whose name means salvation was to marry a prostitute called Gomer and love her. This Hosea did (Hosea 1). Wow! Just imagine God telling you as a prophet to do what He instructed Hosea to do. I can see a lot of Christians who read this suggestion saying, "Well, God told Hosea to do that because He was depicting what Christ (salvation) will do for believers. God will not ask anyone to do something so stupid now, in this dispensation." God may not ask a person to marry a prostitute to depict salvation because Jesus already came; but God can and still does give some people, especially His prophets, instructions that enact the message that He wants to pass across to His people. Sometimes these enactments make sense, and sometimes they do not.

A prophet has to trust the instruction received and obey them to the latter. I remember one prayer meeting that our ministry had, and God gave one of those "not making sense" instructions of a prophetic enactment. The instruction was for us to lie on the floor as we were praying, and roll around on the ground seven times for that specific prayer request that we were interceding for. At first I did not want to give the instruction that God gave me because it did not make sense to me, and so I wondered how it would sound and seem to others. Think for a moment about Hosea's instructions to marry a prostitute, note that in Hosea's time people's perception of morality was very stringent and different. Marrying a prostitute definitely questioned his position as a man of God, as well as his judgment of morality. It must not have been easy for Hosea to marry Gomer, but he did. Also, it was not easy for me to tell the other people at the prayer meeting that we were to lay on our sides and roll from one end of the room to another while we prayed. But I said it, we did it, and testimonies followed. The point that I am trying to pass across is that as a prophet, there will be times that God will give instructions, especially, during intercession that will not make sense. But as long as there is no shadow of doubt in your mind, obey, and if you are in any doubt, wait until you are sure. You might ask, what if the instruction is contrary to scripture? Then it is not the LORD that has given that instruction because God's words do not contradict itself. However, we need to be careful that our guideline is scripture and not traditions and culture. For the Bible says that our traditions and culture has made the word of God not to be effective.

If Hosea had considered tradition and culture, he would never have married Gomer because the traditions and culture of the people frowned on such a union. Hosea considered the word of God instead. His obedience to his assignment emboldened him to preach repentance to the people even more. A practical example of God's love demonstrated through his marriage to Gomer created an avenue for the people to know that they still can be loved by God, regardless of what they have done. So like Hosea, prophets and prophetesses are to be sensitive to God's voice always and be ready to obey the commands and instructions that they hear even to their own discomfort or ridicule by others.

The Prophets Elijah and Elisha

These two prophets are amongst the most powerful in the Old Testament. Surprisingly they do not have a book of their own, but they had very great prophetic mantles with signs and miracles following their ministries. They both commanded fear and respect from the Nation of Israel to which God called them, and their fame was heard across the borders of their nation. Both of these prophets were the leaders of the sons of the prophets in their time, (an assignment that involved training people called to the prophetic office) as well as chief prophets to the nation of Israel.

These prophets called down fire from heaven (1 Kings 18:36-38; 2 Kings 1:10-12), healed bitter waters and barren land (2 Kings 2:19-21), raised the dead (1 Kings 17:19-22; 2 Kings 4:18-37), and made iron to float in water (2 Kings 6:1-7). They no doubt demonstrated the power of God in their lives. There is a lot to learn from their obedience to their great assignments as well as from their weaknesses.

Elijah

He was prophet between 875-848 BC, during the reign of King Ahab of Israel. Elijah was a prophet to be reckoned with; I believe that anyone who decrees that there would be no rain (1 Kings 17:1; 1 Kings 18:1) for any period of time, and it comes to pass, is one to be reckoned with. This was Elijah, the man that troubled Israel (1Kings 18:17), though it was good trouble because it was to warn Israel of their sin. Have you as a prophet ever been accused of troubling anyone because you are constantly sent by God to them? Well you are not alone. The Apostle Paul and his entourage were also accused of a similar offence: of turning the world upside down (Acts 17:1-6). If that is not the same as trouble; then I don't know what is. But any persecution for the sake of the work of ministry is really a feather to one's hat. So rejoice in persecution.

Elijah's ministry was slightly different from most of the other prophets in that God used him a lot to minister to the nation as well as individuals. Most of the other prophets for example: Ezekiel, Jeremiah, Micah, and Isaiah to mention a few were sent to the nation of Israel/Judah as a whole, or to their kings only. But Elijah ministered one-on-one to the people. In first Kings 17:8-24, God sent him to the woman of Zarephath with an instruction for her to feed him. In the same chapter, her son died and Elijah raised him up by the power of the LORD. He also was the head of a school of prophets, which further emphasizes his one-on-one ministration because he served as their mentor. His assignment to individuals is mirrored by that which is in operation today in the prophetic office. Most of the prophets and prophetesses in this dispensation, minister one on one a lot more than to kings and nations though there are some with such assignments. Elijah was a famous, powerful, and very dramatic prophet, yet he had weaknesses as do all people.

One of Elijah's weaknesses was fear. As a prophet, we cannot allow or afford to be too emotional because this will clad our judgment and most importantly, hinder our ability to hear God when He speaks to us, or gives an assignment. Elijah's demonstration of fear when Jezebel threatened to kill him right after he made all the prophets of Baal and Asherah meet their demise, shows that Elijah is only human, but God chooses to work through him. This should serve as a self-image check for any prophet who becomes so "big headed" in him or herself, thinking, because God speaks through them, they have become more spiritual than everyone else. All that God does through one has nothing to do with our ability or "super spirituality." If

Elijah did all or any of the miracles by his power, then he would not have been afraid of Jezebel at any point in time. When he was threatened, I believe that the anointing by which he slew Baal's prophets had lifted (God anoints for specific assignments) so his natural self became afraid. It is important that the prophet knows when there is an anointing for a specific task. You might wonder, *if a prophet is called and released into their office, isn't he already anointed?* Yes, he or she is already anointed to be a prophet. However, there is different and specific anointing for different task within the call, and it takes wisdom to know this. Let us take an example. The prophet Moses; already called to lead Israel to the promise land, still asked God to show him His glory (presence) after all the moves of God that he had seen. Moses refused to go to the promise land any further except God's presence went with Him (Exodus 33:12-18). All Moses was really saying was God anoint me again for this assignment.

Whenever God instructs me to have an event, a crusade, a retreat, or any other type of assignment; I always pray for the anointing to do that assignment. I do not say, "Well, I am already anointed as a prophetess so that is taken care of." No, I ask God to prepare me for this new task, as well as anoint me afresh for it. That way, I do not speak my own words or minister in my own ability. Also, asking for a fresh anointing makes me more sensitive to the Holy Spirit, which eradicates the probability of errors. It is imperative that the prophet knows when the anointing to operate in the gifts of the prophetic office lifts or he will minister in error. When we do not feel the anointing to prophesy, do not let anyone pressure you to speak.

Elijah became afraid of Jezebel. We must not be afraid of any spirit of Jezebel—that is the spirit of manipulation, that spirit that tries to make the prophet or the people of God, especially those in leadership positions to err. I am talking about that person that tries to put the prophet in a situation that says, "If you are a true prophet, then what is God saying about this and that" or "I have come to enquire of the LORD, what is God saying about me?" or "We are inviting you to a conference and we want you to prophesy to everybody." These are examples of situations that can place a prophet on the spot and pressure him to act. If one is not careful, fear of being termed false, or the fear of not being respected, as well as other types of fear arises within and mistakes are made—mistake of operating in self and not according to the word of the LORD.

A true prophet or prophetess of God cannot allow him or her self to be manipulated in any way, because you are a spokesman for God alone and not for man. When fear comes, turn it over to the LORD. Ask for a fresh unction of anointing that gives you strength to face and accomplish the task. If Elijah had asked God for the anointing to deal with Jezebel, he would never have run away. So do not run away either whenever you feel depleted, God is always available to replenish you.

Elisha

Elisha, the son of Shepphat, anointed with double portion of Elijah's anointing, and chief prophet during his reign served as prophet between 848-797 BC. He was prophet to four kings of Israel: Joram, Jehu, Jehoahaz, and Jehoash. Like Elijah, Elisha was also a prophet with a great mantle, and he ministered one on one to the people; for example, to the wife of the sons of the prophet and to the Shunammite woman (2 Kings 4). As aforementioned, he performed many miracles in his time and was greatly respected by all. However, he also demonstrated some weakness, which every prophet should learn from. Elisha had some anger issues.

The Bible tells us of a very interesting event that occurred on Elisha's way back from Jericho to Bethel. He just finished performing the miracle of healing bitter waters and a barren land. One would think that he was still filled with God's anointing considering what just happened, and as such he should have his emotions in check. Alas, that was not the case. For as Elisha went up to Bethel, some young children mocked him that he had a bald head, and Elisha killed them. Yes, he did. He cursed the children in the name of the LORD and two she bears came out of the woods and killed all forty-two of them (2 Kings 2:23-25). Wow! Is that anger issues or what? My belief is that Elisha killed the poor children for nothing, and it also was a major abuse of anointing and power. After all they were kids and could have been warned or corrected.

It is important that every born again believer takes a lesson from this, for the power of death and life is in the tongue, so we should be careful to use the tongue to bless and not to curse. The prophets should take double heed of this advice because of the anointing that rest on the office. Although every believer who understands his authority in Christ has the power to decree a thing and it is so, the prophet has this power twice over when the anointing of the office rest on him for a specific task.

Therefore, when the anointing to operate the gifts of the office is sensed (for every prophet knows when that auction is upon them), it is imperative that we do not allow any emotion to interfere with the assignment that is given. We are to be focused and act, not react to situations that anger us. Elisha reacted to the children's taunting. An action would mean that he had time to think about the best way to handle the children, and I believe it would not have been death. Acting instead of reacting would allow us to do that which will glorify God's name at all times, and the prophetic office will not be tainted. God is merciful and will continue to use His prophets as long as we are yielding even when we sometimes make mistakes. Also, God's gifts and callings are without repentance. This means that God does not withdraw His anointing and gifts very easily or quickly. However, God's desire for us is to declare and deliver His words in love and compassion and not out of anger, hurt, pain, or from our own selfish reasons or ambitions.

Apart from anger issues, Elisha also demonstrated bulging under pressure. The Bible records that after Elijah was taken by a whirlwind to heaven, the sons of the prophets wanted to go and search for him. They obviously did not believe that he was neither dead nor left behind somewhere on the mountains. But Elisha knew better than that. He knew that his master had gone to heaven and that was why he told the sons of the prophets not to look for him. But he allowed them to influence his faith and eventually changed his original instruction (2 Kings 2:15-18). That Elisha changed his original instruction is bad enough, but the reason that made him change it, is worse.

> And when they urged him till he was ashamed,
> he said, send. They sent therefore fifty men;
> and they sought three days, but found him not.
> 2 Kings 2:17

The reason that influenced Elisha to change his instruction was shame. The question is ashamed of what? Ashamed that the people thought he did not care about his master and mentor? Ashamed that Elijah would think he did not care about his where about peradventure he was on top of the mountains? Or Elisha was ashamed because he was the only one saying that Elijah would not be found (after all, the others were prophets also). Whatever the reason was that made Elisha ashamed, it overthrew his better judgment. Here again we find emotion in flinching on what was otherwise settled in his mind.

A prophet cannot afford to doubt that which was already spoken to him or that which was perceived in the spirit realm, except it is not yet settled in him. Again we see why a prophet is to prophesy according to his proportion of faith, anything that is not of faith is sin according to scriptures. So if the word that you perceive is not settled in you, do not speak, or you will speak in error or make mistakes. If the word is settled in your spirit, then speak and trust it even if it does not make you win the popularity contest.

The Prophets Micaiah and Jehu

The prophet Micaiah's ministry was around 853 BC. It can be said that both Micaiah and Jehu's ministries had minor assignments compared to the likes of Elijah, Elisha, and Jeremiah to mention a few. Micaiah and Jehu are examples of prophets without major assignment, but yet they were sent to kings. By not having a major assignment, they were not sent to the kings as often as Jeremiah was neither were they used by God to deliver "countless" prophecies to the nation of Israel or Judah, but rather, God would send them now and then with a word to a king or a person. However, their ministries were just as important as all the other prophets, because they delivered the word of God.

Micaiah

Micaiah was one of the prophets during the reign of Ahab of Israel and Jehoshaphat of Judah. These kings were to go into battle with Ramoth-gilead and they wanted to know what God's will for them was; so they sought out the prophet Micaiah (1 Kings 22 and 2 Chronicles 18).

> And Jehoshaphat said, is there not here a prophet of the LORD besides, that we might enquire of him.
>
> 1 Kings 22:7

God—contrary to what some ministers believe —still sends His prophets to give answers to His people, when they inquire from Him, even today. The argument that these ministers or believers raise is that in the New Testament, The Holy Spirit is indwelling the Christian and all the answers that are needed can be told to the person inwardly in his spirit by the Holy Ghost.

There is no problem with this rationale that the Holy Spirit does speak to the believer and answers our questions. The only issue with this is that; most of the time when the Holy Spirit is speaking to us, we do not hear Him. Either we are not sensitive enough to hear, or we ignore Him even when we hear. At other times, the Holy Spirit just did not give the answer to the person who asked the question. So these circumstances can warrant God to speak through His prophets. After all, God set the prophets to be His mouthpiece. This function in the Old Testament, did not change in the New, otherwise, Jesus would not have given this gift (Ephesians 4) to the body of Christ.

The Prophet Jehu

Jehu functioned as prophet between 865-853 BC mostly in the same manner as Micaiah, that is, God occasionally sent him with a prophetic word to the king (1 Kings 16:1-7 and 2 Chronicles 19:1-3). Most prophets in the New Testament church fall into the type of prophetic function of Micaiah and Jehu. God on occasions sent them to someone with a word; very few people have prophetic mantles of the likes of Jeremiah and Ezekiel. This is due to the fact that in the time of these prophets, sin was very rampant, and there was no atonement for sin because Christ had not yet come, died, and resurrected. So God had to constantly send His prophets to warn, instruct, and correct the people so that they will not be destroyed. But now, the New Testament believer has the Holy Spirit (as discussed earlier) to correct and to teach us. God, therefore, sends His prophets much less to His people. This explains why we do not see many prophets crying in the streets "repent, repent, or be destroyed." Instead the ministry is more subtle, yet very functional.

The Prophets Ahijah and Nathan

These prophets had ministries similar to that of Micaiah and Jehu, which makes them different from Jeremiah and the likes. God used them to minister one on one to individuals as well as kings to call them to order, but not to Israel as a nation. The prophet Ahijah was sent to King Jeroboam to tell him that the kingdom of Israel would be taken from the hand of King Solomon and divided into two and that he would be king over one of them (1 Kings 11:29-32). In 1 Kings 14, Ahijah was sought out by king Jeroboam to hear the word of the LORD when his son became sick. Examples of other prophets with Ahijah, Jehu, and Micaiah's type of ministry in having minor assignments are: Hanani the seer (2 Chronicles 16), whom God sent to King Asa when he did not trust God to deliver him form the king of Syria; Hananiah who gave a false prophetic word to King Zedekiah (Jeremiah 28); Gad, the seer, who was sent to David when he numbered Israel and sinned against God (1 Chronicles 21:1-15; and the prophet Nathan who was prophet to King David.

Nathan who also falls into this category of not been a major prophet, did not perform any miracles, signs, or wonders; however, he had a great ministry, which was to the king (not the subjects), and he excelled in that which God committed to him. He was bold to correct or chastise the king when it was needed, but he did it with wisdom as led of the LORD. For example, when David took Uriah's wife and killed him, Nathan was sent to confront David of his sin (2 Samuel 12). Nathan spoke to David in parables that helped to soften and prepare David to receive the LORD's chastening. Now, Nathan could have rebuked David without respecting him as king, but this was not the case. Nathan never forgot that David was king though he was the prophet; neither did David forget that Nathan was God's spokesman. They had mutual respect for one another.

There are times that God will use a prophet to rebuke or correct a person in high governmental or monarchial authority. Contrary to what many believe, God still does this to this day. The important point for all prophets to remember is that when God does this, he also orchestrates exactly how the word is to be delivered. God understands authority (for He created it), and He is all about honor and respect. It is always beneficial to the prophet to deliver a word to anybody exactly as the LORD order's it because this influences the recipient's ability to believe the word and act on it, except the recipient has decided not to heed God's Word.

Pre-exilic Prophets to Judah

These pre-exilic prophets had their primary assignments to Judah, although they occasionally had a prophetic word about other nations. They also had their strengths and pitfalls, and there are several lessons to be learnt from both their lives and ministries.

The Prophet Joel

Joel was the son of Pethuel, and served as prophet approximately between 835-796 BC. His audience was

Judah where Joash had just become king. The people of Judah as it had become a tradition for them, intermittently would forget God and start the worshipping of idols. So God sent them Joel to set them on the right path with very strong metaphorical corrections.

The word of the LORD that came to Joel the son of Pethuel. Hear this, ye old men, and give ear, all ye inhabitants of the land. Hath this been in your days, or even in the days of your fathers? Tell ye your children of it, and let your children tell their children, and their children another generation. That which the palmerworm hath left hath the locust eaten; and that which the locust hath left hath the cankerworm eaten; and that which the cankerworm hath left hath the caterpillar eaten. Awake, ye drunkards, and weep; and howl, all ye drinkers of wine, because of the new wine; for it is cut off from your mouth. For a nation is come up upon my land, strong, and without number, whose teeth are the teeth of a lion, and he hath the cheek teeth of a great lion. He hath laid my vine waste, and barked my fig tree: he hath made it clean bare, and cast it away; the branches thereof are made white. Lament like a virgin girded with sackcloth for the husband of her youth. The meat offering and the drink offering is cut off from the house of the LORD; the priests, the LORD's ministers, mourn. The field is wasted, the land mourneth; for the corn is wasted: the new wine is dried up, the oil languisheth. Be ye ashamed, O ye husbandmen; howl, O ye vinedressers, for the wheat and for the barley; because the harvest of the field is perished. The vine is dried up, and the fig tree languisheth; the pomegranate tree, the palm tree also, and the apple tree even all the trees of the field, are withered: because joy is withered away from the sons of men. Gird yourselves, and lament, ye priests: howl, ye ministers of the altar: come, lie all night in sackcloth, ye ministers of my God: for the meat offering and the drink offering is with holden from the house of your God.

Sanctify ye a fast, call a solemn assembly, gather the elders and all the inhabitants of the land into the house of the LORD your God, and cry unto the LORD, Alas for the day! for the day of the LORD is at hand, and as a destruction from the Almighty shall it come. Is not the meat cut off before our eyes, yea, joy and gladness from the house of our God? The seed is rotten under their clods, the garners are laid desolate, the barns are broken down; for the corn is withered. How do the beasts groan! the herds of cattle are perplexed, because they have no pasture; yea, the flocks of sheep are made desolate. O LORD, to thee will I cry: for the fire hath devoured the pastures of the wilderness, and the flame hath burned all the trees of the field. The beasts of the field cry also unto thee: for the rivers of waters are dried up, and the fire hath devoured the pastures of the wilderness.

Joel 1

Joel is an example of how God can speak to His people about their sins in very dramatic terms: "the vine is dried up," "the apple tree lanquisheth." What in the world does that mean? Why did God not just tell them what their sin was in plain words? You see, sometimes God uses metaphors, similes, and allegory to speak to us to bring the message to us more clearly. He uses comparisons, parables, and examples for better understanding in order for us to know the depth of the matter. God did that in the Old Testament and also in the New (Jesus who is the ultimate prophet once told us to beware of those who come in sheep's clothing, but inside are ravening wolves). In this statement, right away the hearer pictures someone whose gentle or calm look is deceptive. He does not picture a sheep with the insides of a wolf. In the same manner when God uses a figure of speech in a prophetic word it is because that is the best way for the recipient to perceive what God is bringing across. As a prophet, there will be times when the word of God in your mouth will come out in figures of speech. Be not afraid of how it sounds or whether it makes sense or not, as long as you know you heard from God, there is nothing to be afraid of or worried about.

Joel had an assignment of calling the people to repentance and warning them of the approaching judgment (Joel 1 and 2:1-26). In addition, he spoke of the day of the coming of the LORD's spirit upon His people. I believe that this is Joel's most important ministration, because in those days the spirit of the LORD did not stay on the earth realm. It comes on someone and then lifts. But Joel prophesied that all would partake of God's spirit. This was new to the people in that dispensation, and so it must have taken boldness on the part of Joel to declare such words.

> And it shall come to past afterward, that I will pour out my Spirit upon all flesh; and your sons and daughters shall prophesy, your old men shall dream dreams, your young men shall see visions: And also upon thee servants and upon the handmaids in those days will I pour out my spirit.
>
> Joel 2:28-29

Joel spoke these words as the LORD gave him utterance. He did not try to rationalize how God can or will pour His spirit upon all flesh (Jews and non Jews alike). What is your assignment to the body of Christ? Does it need much boldness to perform it? Is it new? Does it sound different? Well, take lessons from Joel, declare the word that is placed in your mouth or perform the task that is given to you. As long as it is not contrary to scriptural principles (so you must be conversant with the Bible, and it is wisdom to have spiritual counsel from godly people whom you know, and they know you), go ahead and fulfill your God-given assignment in life and do not allow circumstances to deter you.

The Prophet Isaiah

Isaiah's prophetic ministry was between 740-681 BC. He was prophet during the reign of kings Uzziah, Jotham, Ahaz, Hezekiah, and Manasseh. His audience was primarily Judah, but he also spoke to Israel. He was prophet when the nation of Israel had sinned, and Judah was beginning to follow in Israel's footsteps. So God sent him to Judah to call them back to Him. The book of Isaiah contains the message of pointing out the people's sin and God's judgment for sin. This message is typical of most of the other prophet's assignment. Isaiah, however, had another very specific message to declare; one that was peculiar to his ministry although some other prophets touched it lightly. It was the message of redemption and salvation, a message of the soon coming suffering Messiah and conquering king. It was the message of one that will have an everlasting kingdom. This was the assignment of Isaiah that was different from the others. Examples of some of the messianic prophecies that were given by Isaiah are:

> Behold, a virgin shall conceive, and bear a son, and shall call his name Immanuel.
>
> Isaiah 7:14b

> The people that walked in darkness have seen a great light: they that dwell in the land of the shadow of death, upon them hath the light shined.
>
> Isaiah 9:2

For unto us a child is born, unto us a son is given: and the government shall be upon His shoulder: and His name shall be called Wonderful, Counsellor, The mighty God, The everlasting Father, The Prince of Peace.

Isaiah 9:6

And there shall come forth a rod out of the stem of Jesse, and a Branch shall grow out of his roots: And the Spirit of the LORD shall rest upon him, the spirit of wisdom and understanding, the spirit of counsel and might, the spirit of knowledge and of the fear of the LORD.

Isaiah 11:1-2

Isaiah gave these prophecies a long time before Jesus was born. Imagine if he was afraid to speak or write them down because they sounded weird and strange. You know, a virgin giving birth, a king that will live forever and have an everlasting kingdom? How is that possible? That is what some prophets might have said if God had commissioned them to speak the same words. Because a given word does not make sense to the natural mind, does not mean that it is not God speaking. As long as the word that you hear is not against God, then wait on it if you are confused or not clear. Ask God to make it clear and give you the ability to believe it, even if it does not make sense, so that you can deliver it. If Isaiah had refused to speak the prophecy about Jesus, God would have had to use someone else because these prophecies were non-personal (chapter four); therefore, they needed to be told and they must come to pass. Isaiah would have missed a huge part of his assignment if he had spoken every other prophecy and left these ones out. Every prophet has to be cautious not to leave out any part of their assignments because you do not know which one is the most important of all of them.

The Prophet Micah

Micah served as prophet between 742-687 BC during the reign of kings Jotham, Ahaz, and Hezekiah of Judah. Micah's audience included the people of Samaria and Jerusalem as well as all Israel and Judah. During Micah's ministry, Isaiah and Hosea were also serving as prophets. As was generally common to all the prophets, repentance was also the message of Micah's ministry. The people at this time were into idol worship (Micah 1:7) amongst other sins, and the worst of all was that the prophets who were supposed to correct them were also involved in sin. So the LORD sent Micah not just to rebuke the people but the prophets as well.

> Thus said the LORD concerning the prophets that make my people err, that bite with their teeth, and cry peace; and he that putteth not unto their mouths, they even prepare war against him. Therefore night shall be unto you, that ye shall not have a vision; and it shall be dark into you, that you shall not divine; and the sun shall go down over the prophets, and

the day shall be dark over them. Then shall
the seers be ashamed, even the diviners con-
founded: yea, they shall all cover their lips; for
there is no answer of God.

Micah 3:5-7

This was Micah, a prophet, rebuking other prophets for dancing to the people's tune instead of that of
God's. It must have looked hypocritical to the other
prophets for one of their own to come against them,
and for them to be chastised the same time with the
diviners. That must have been embarrassing for them.
But Micah's assignment was clear to him. God had put
a word in his mouth and it was to be spoken just as he
was told. In fact Micah demonstrated his boldness and
his zeal to obey only God as seen in the verse below.

But truly I am full of the power by the Spirit
of the LORD, and of judgment, and of might,
to declare unto Jacob his transgression, and to
Israel his sin.

Micah 3:8

Micah left no room for doubt in the minds of all who
heard him that he knew he was a true prophet of God
and that he would declare the truth so help him God.

This prophet's ministry gives a good example that
God can and does use prophets to correct one another.
So let no one in this office think that he or she is above
or beyond rebuke by one of his or her own. It takes
a very mature prophet to receive a rebuke from God

through another prophet, especially from one that is "younger" in the prophetic office (humility is also required on the part of the younger prophet to deliver the word, for God to use him again in that capacity). But this is where those called to this office need to be very careful and not become pious and prideful when God gives a work that involves speaking a word of correction, chastisement, rebuke, or even encouragement to one another. Whenever humility is taken away from the lifestyle of one called to this office, nothing, but destruction and an unfulfilled prophetic ministry remains.

The Prophet Obadiah

Scholars say that there are two possible dates for Obadiah's prophetic ministry 853-841 BC, which places his ministry around the same time with that of Elijah, Jehu, and Miciah or 627-586 BC, which was during Jeremiah's reign as prophet. The most important aspect to this study, however, is his assignment. It was to Edom and Jerusalem. The children of Esau (Edomites) were constantly at loggerheads with God's people whom they persecuted (Obadiah 1:6-14). So God sent them Obadiah.

God's message through this prophet is the type of message that every, and anyone would like to hear whenever a prophetic word is given. You know the kind that declares war on your enemies and prosperity on you, the kind that have words of encouragement and God's blessings alone, without any repentance or judgmental messages attached. That was the kind of assignment that Obadiah had for Jerusalem.

> And thy mighty men, O Teman, shall be dismayed, to the end that every one on the mount of Esau may be cut off by slaughter. For thy violence against thy brother Jacob shame shall cover thee, and thou shalt be cut off for ever.
> Obadiah 1:9-10

> But upon mount Zion shall be deliverance, and there shall be holiness; and the house of Jacob shall possess their possessions. And the house of Jacob shall be a fire, and the house of Joseph a flame, and the house of Esau for stubble, and they shall kindle in them, and devour them; and there shall not be any remaining of the house of Esau; for the LORD hath spoken it.
> Obadiah 1:17-18

As a prophetess, I can tell you that this is the type of assignment that 90 percent of prophets would want to give. The type that makes us look good at all times, the one that does not "ruffle any feathers," or need much courage to speak forth or perform. Well, Obadiah had it a little easy (that is not to say that there may not have been other words that were harshly spoken, which are not recorded in scriptures), but going with the prophecy that scripture records, Obadiah must have been liked, because he spoke what Israel wanted to hear.

The majority of people in the church today will endorse Obadiah as a true prophet and call the likes of Jeremiah and Ezekiel false because of the differences in their messages. But unfortunately or fortunately, all prophets do not have Obadiah's kind of message alone. It is usually mixed with repentance, corrections, instructions, rebukes, and encouragements. We should remember that Obadiah spoke to two nations, Israel and Edom, and for the Edomites, the prophetic word was not good, in fact it was judgment. What was applauded by Israel was definitely frowned upon by the other nation.

The Prophet Nahum

The Prophet Nahum is believed to have been prophet in Judah from 663-612 BC. He was a contemporary of Zephaniah. Manasseh was the king during Nahum's ministry and his audiences were both Judah and the Assyrians. Nahum's assignment was slightly different from that of most prophets; God did not send him with a message of repentance, rather with one of comfort. This comfort came to Judah from the prophecies about the Assyrians of what God was going to do to them because of their wickedness (Nahum 1, 2 and 3).

The Assyrians were the world power at that time with their capital at Nineveh. They were arrogant and oppressive and they had great military strength. They conquered Israel the Northern kingdom and made Judah to pay tribute to them. The people of Nineveh at this time had completely forgotten God who had sent them a prophet (Jonah) a hundred years earlier telling them that they would be destroyed because of their sin.

The Assyrians obviously had no respect for God, or His power. If they did they would not have troubled God's people. So Nahum was sent to them with a word of judgment with no opportunity to repent because the Babylonians came and destroyed Assyria. God usually sends His prophets and prophetesses to His people, although sometimes God will send a word to an unbelieving nation or person. The book of Nahum (like the book of Jonah) is an example of God sending a prophet to a people who do not know Him. That is a people or person who does not serve the LORD. Therefore, when a prophet finds that he has a burden to intercede or go and deliver a word to a Muslim, or a pagan nation, it should not be strange or scary to him.

The Prophet Zephaniah

The prophet Zephaniah was contemporary of Jeremiah. He served as prophet to Judah from 640–621 BC when Josiah was king. The Bible does not tell us how he was called, except that he was the son of Cushi, and great, great grandson of Hizkiah.

During the time of Zephaniah's ministry, the people of Judah had not repented of their sin of forsaking God and going after other gods. They worshipped Baal, Molech, and the stars in heaven. Judah at this time had economic stability, and a good king who actually feared God; but the people had no need for God anymore. What? With the wealth and security that they had, the people had become complacent. Zephaniah's assignment was to remind the people that God was not happy with them and that they had need of repentance or face destruction.

Have you ever been accused as a prophet, to be one of doom? You know, always prophesying judgment upon the people? Well, fret no longer, you have one example amongst other prophets that is mentioned in the scriptures. Zephaniah prophesied all kinds of God's judgment upon Judah. Unlike Habakkuk who kept asking God questions about why His judgment was tarring, Zephaniah declared destruction. But that was how he was instructed to deliver the word from God. A prophet is a mouthpiece of God even in these days and he or she must not be afraid to declare what God is speaking. Throughout Zephaniah chapters 1–3:8, the prophecies of doom are recorded. But praise God that He is also merciful, because verses 3:9-20 tell of God's deliverance if the people repent. It is filled with hope and restoration.

The question may be asked that when God sends a prophet to give a word of judgment to a person, must the prophecy also have a word of restoration in it. The answer to this is that it depends on the circumstances that led to the message being delivered in the first place. By this I mean that God handles each situation differently. God gives us many chances to repent from our sins, but if we keep turning a deaf ear, then one day we may receive a prophecy of doom with no chance to repent; or even if we do repent, the consequences of our action remains. Let us consider this example: Jeremiah gave a prophecy to King Zedekiah that he will be taken to Babylon, and he and his house shall not live except he submits to the Kingdom of Babylon (Jeremiah 38:17-20). Now what kind of a word is that to a king, to tell him to allow himself to be taken captive and be subject to another king? Zedekiah did not listen, as will a lot of people today, to whom God might send such similar (crazy) instructions. So what happened to Zedekiah? He was taken to Babylon, which was inevitable because it was already in God's plan for Judah to go into captivity for their unrepentant sin. But Zedekiah's eyes would not have been plucked out, nor his children killed (Jeremiah 52:8-11) if he had obeyed God and submitted to Babylon (Zedekiah had a chance not to be totally destroyed, but he did not take it).

Asa is another example of a king who received a prophecy of doom through Hanani the seer. In Asa's case war was prophesied to him for the remaining of his days because he had relied on the king of Syria to help him fight a war, with Baasha, king of Israel, instead of relying on God (2 Chronicles 16:7-9). In another situation, Asa became sick and instead of seeking God for healing, he consulted the physicians. God was angry at this and He allowed Asa to die (2 Chronicles 16: 12). As a prophet, there maybe times where God will require a difficult word to be given as in these cited cases. But be assured that when God does this, it is because the recipient has turned a deaf ear to subsequent warnings, corrections, and instructions from God. The sad thing though is that the audience who hears the prophetic word of doom for someone may not know, how long, or how many times God has sent corrective words to the person, but to no avail. All that the audience heard is the prophet's word of doom, which came at the last stage, with no chance for the person to repent. So it becomes easy for the prophet to be persecuted and termed false. Because the people will say that God will not destroy a person without a chance to make amends. But no matter the persecution, it should not deter the prophet from his or her assignment; they should deliver the word so that God will not hold them responsible at any point in time.

The Prophet Jeremiah

Jeremiah is a good example that a prophet is called before they are born (Jeremiah 1:1-4). He served as a prophet to the kingdom of Judah from 627 BC until the exile in 586 BC. Although Jeremiah was called before he was born, he did not know that until he had an encounter with God concerning his calling.

> Then the LORD put forth his hand, and touched my mouth. And the LORD said unto me, behold, I have put my words in thy mouth. See, I have this day set thee over the nations and over the kingdoms, to root out, and to pull down, and to destroy, and to throw down, to build, and to plant.
>
> Jeremiah 1:9-10

On the day of this encounter, Jeremiah was officially released into his ministry, and his ministry assignment was given to him. In the same manner, when God calls someone into the prophetic or any other ministerial office, God will tell you. He will either tell you himself, through other prophets or ministers, or both. And He may or not give you your assignment immediately.

Jeremiah was prophet in the time when the society was fast deteriorating spiritually, economically, and politically. The people of Judah did not want to hear about God. So Jeremiah's assignment was to remind them of God and bring their sins to their knowledge. This he was to do by rooting, pulling, destroying, and tearing down. Simply put, he was to point out their faults. The people of Judah were disloyal. They forsook God, burned incense to other gods, worshiped the works of their hands, and exchanged God for other things (Jeremiah 1:16, 3, 7, and 18). This sin, Jeremiah told them to repent of, or God will punish them (Jeremiah 11, 13, 14, 16, and 25). Jeremiah was not to stop at just pointing out their sins; he was also to tell the people that God can and would restore them if they repented (Jeremiah 30, 31, 32, and 33). That is why he was to build and to plant. In other words, he was also to give them hope that all was not lost and that God is merciful and forgiving.

However, they did not listen to him, instead he was persecuted. Just as it is in this day: when a prophet delivers a word, especially if it has to do with repentance from hidden sins or corrections where someone has done things his own way; majority of the body of Christ do not listen. They instead persecute the prophet. But that should not stop any true prophet from continuing in the assignment. I remember some cases where God had sent me to give words of corrections or instructions to some ministers. They did not listen, but called it all kinds of name that is not worth mentioning. But thank God that the words came to pass.

In this office of a prophet, I have come to realize that the most difficult people to receive a word from God are people in ministry or people who believe that they have been saved longer than you. They forget that it is not you the prophet that is speaking, but God who called you to that office. But just like Jeremiah, you do not give up or run away and hide.

Jeremiah did not relent. He understood that God had anointed and ordained him for this purpose and it did not matter which king was ruling (he served the last five kings) he delivered his God given message, especially to the kings. Jeremiah was a great prophet with a great mantle and his prophecies came to pass. He was very bold and yet was known as the weeping prophet (Jeremiah 9), because he was so sorrowful for the fallen condition of God's people in Judah. He wrote the book of Jeremiah as well as the book of Lamentations.

The Prophet Habakkuk

The prophet Habakkuk was prophet in Judah about 612–589 BC, the same time as Jeremiah. He too saw the wicked act of the people in forsaking their God for other gods. He was also aware of the political and economic state of the kingdom. But unlike Jeremiah whose assignment was to urge the people to repentance, Habakkuk's assignment was birthed out of his burden. His burden was for the evil of the people to be punished.

As Jeremiah warned the people of the impending danger of being taken captive by the Babylonians, Habakkuk wondered why God was taking so long in teaching the people of Judah a lesson for their sins. Out of this burden, Habakkuk cried to God. This is a classical example of a prophet and intercession. The book of Habakkuk is filled with questions or prayer of petition (Habakkuk 1:1-4, 12-17) and God's reply to them (Habakkuk 1:5-11, 2:2-20). After which Habakkuk praised God for hearing and answering his questions (Habakkuk 3).

Habakkuk did more praying than prophesying. This was the nature of his work. All prophets should be intercessors. We should be concerned when things are going wrong around us and in our nation. And like Habakkuk, we should take it to God in prayer. Although, Habakkuk wanted judgment, we should pray the people to also repent. So the next time you find that you have a strong burden for something good or bad, you have the responsibility of praying it to happen if it is for good, or praying it to stop if it is something bad.

It is also allowed to go to God with questions, no matter how crazy it might seem. Sometimes as prophets, we observe things that are happening in our society, church, or homes, and it bothers us, and yet nobody else seems to care about it. They may not even see it as a problem or an issue. At other times, we sense things in the spiritual realm that need urgent attention in prayer, which other people may not sense. At times like this, we are on an assignment to intercede. And it is imperative that we do not joke or play with it or we will be disobedient to our call. Like Habakkuk, we should take it to God in prayer.

Exilic And Post-exilic Prophets

The exilic prophets ministered to God's people while they were in exile in Babylon. Their main message was to remind the captives of their loyalty to God before anyone else. Like the name implies, the post-exilic prophets had their ministry after the exile. Whether exilic or post-exilic, there are situations and circumstances that occurred in the ministries of these prophets that everyone can learn from, especially those called to the prophetic office.

The Prophet Daniel

Daniel's ministry was between 605-536 BC. This places him around the same time with Ezekiel, Jeremiah and Habakkuk's ministries, which ran concurrently. Daniel was a prophet when the people were in exile in Babylon and he served during the rule of three powerful kings: Nebuchadnezzar and Belshazzar of Babylon and Darius of Medes. Daniel under these kings did not serve as a prophet, but as a wise man in Babylon and as an adviser to Darius the king in Medes. However, to the children of Israel he was regarded as a prophet.

Daniel was not the regular "thus saith the LORD" prophet. Because of this, I am tempted to say that Daniel was more of a powerful intercessor with prophetic insight. Daniel was an interpreter of dreams, some of which he had himself. For this reason, the prophetic ministry of Daniel was different from that of most prophets in the Old Testament. Daniel's ability to interpret dreams and visions gave him a very successful ministry, one so successful that kings called for him to exercise his gifts. Daniel in doing this was fulfilling God's assignment for his life, for God had raised him up to speak His mind to these kings. God set it up in a way that the kings had visions and dreams and desired to know what it meant. That way, when Daniel came with the meanings, they had to know it was from God, since the wise men from their own country did not know the interpretation. So Daniel did not have to say, "Thus saith the LORD," which may not have been received by the king, but an interpretation was received.

Daniel chapter two records the story of King Nebuchadnezzar and the dream he had that he forgot when he woke up. He called his wise men, not just to interpret, but also to recount the dream to him. They did not know how, so he threatened to kill all of them, and Daniel asked for time to seek God and report to him later.

> Then was the secret revealed unto Daniel in a
> night vision. Then Daniel blessed the God of
> heaven.
>
> Daniel 2:19a

God revealed the dream to Daniel while he slept. How awesome. It is important to note that even today God still reveals secrets to His prophets, whether by night vision or any other means.

There are times when God had revealed some secrets to me. I remember one time when God in a dream showed me a couple I know. In the dream, I saw the woman sleeping in the guest room. When I woke up, I asked God what the meaning of the dream was. And He said to me that there was a problem in the couple's marriage, and I was to call them and ask, "Why are you sleeping in different rooms?" So I did what the LORD said, and the wife began to cry and said to me "for you to know this, God must have showed you, because no one knows about it." They decided to get counsel about their marriage, and today they are fine. You might ask? Why will God show a prophet any person's private matters? Well, God is in the business of mending "fences" and feuds. If sending you a prophet is what you need to make you do the right thing, then that is what God will do. That is not to say that God always tells a prophet any and everyone's secret. But there are times that he does and let no one confuse you that he does not anymore.

In the case of Nebuchadnezzar, God sent Daniel to him with the dream, and its interpretation, which was actually a prophecy of what was to come, and it came to pass. In Daniel chapter four, King Nebuchadnezzar had another dream about a tree. He called Daniel to interpret it for him, this time he remembered the dream; but Daniel was reluctant to give the king the meaning of the dream.

> Then Daniel, whose name was Belteshazzar, was astonished for one hour, and his thoughts troubled him. The king spake and said, Belteshazzar, let not the dream, or the interpretation thereof trouble thee.
>
> Daniel 4:19a

He was reluctant because the meaning was not in the king's favor. The king was to be driven from men and to live in the forest with animals. He was to eat grass, and stay in this condition for seven years after which God would restore him back. God was to take Nebuchadnezzar through this, because he had disrespected God. Is it a wonder that Daniel hesitated before he gave the word to the king?

As a prophet, has God ever given you such awkward message, or as in Daniel's case, interpretation to a dream or vision for someone before? Of course I do not mean exactly the same format as in, "you will live like a beast in the forest," but a word that is so hard to speak, that you do not know what to do or how to go about delivering it. I have found myself in such situations more than once, and yes it was very difficult for me to deliver the message, but I did. There are two questions that I always ask myself in such situations: will you obey man or God? And do you fear man or God? Your sincere answer will determine what you do. Daniel esteemed God above all else (this is a known fact, for he chose the lion's den over disrespect for God). He eventually told Nebuchadnezzar the meaning of the dream.

Daniel's ministry was filled with dreams, visions, and their interpretation (Daniel 5, 7, 8, 10, and 12). God spoke to him a lot about the end times, and up till now his visions and dreams are being fulfilled. This prophet had a unique ministry. His specific assignment wasn't one of calling the people to repentance; rather it was one of preparing the people for that which was to come. Every prophet has his or her own specific assignment within the general call. It is wisdom to know that which God has raised you for and to fulfill it instead of trying to be or do that, which is somebody else's, and then leaving your own undone. It is important to note that I am not referring to helping one another in ministry, or wanting to be successful like someone you know in ministry. Instead I am referring to copying another's blueprint for ministry without asking or listening to God for your own.

The Prophet Ezekiel

Ezekiel, the priest and prophet, had his ministry between 593-571 BC. He was prophet to the Jews in captivity in Babylon (he was taken to Babylon in 597 BC). His ministry parallels those of Daniel, also in Babylon, and Jeremiah in Judah. The main message of his ministry like most prophets was that of repentance. Ezekiel preached to the exiles in Babylon to repent of their sins, he prophesied about the approaching destruction of Jerusalem and also prophesied to the surrounding nations that mocked God on not being powerful enough to deliver His people. But the most exciting part of Ezekiel's ministry, one that was quite different from others and worthy to note are these: the way he was called, and his method of ministration.

God showed Ezekiel a vision of four living creatures and the wheel, and the appearance of the likeness of His glory (Ezekiel 1) when Ezekiel did not yet know that he was called to be a prophet. It was after the vision that God revealed to him who he was in chapter 2. Sometimes God uses dramatic means to let us know our calling; Ezekiel probably thought he was only to be a priest, but God had other plans for him. Have you as a minister been preparing for an office only to find out, that there were more responsibilities than you expected? Or that the office you were prepared for is a preamble to your real calling? Or that the office you have been in was the wrong one. Well, Ezekiel did not go into the wrong office as a priest, but there sure was more for him than he anticipated. It will not be presumptuous to say that Ezekiel's preparation for the position of a priest also prepared him for the office of a prophet. His commitment and dedication to his responsibilities as priest showed that he could be trusted in other areas. And soon enough, God made known to him his other calling. It is important as a child of God to take whatever position we find ourselves in the course of life very seriously, because we do not know what God has set as a stepping-stone toward our calling. How we handle the different responsibilities that are given to us at any present time set precedence for greater responsibilities. Ezekiel did well as priest, and it shouldn't be surprising that he also was successful as prophet.

Ezekiel's ministry was filled with visions and very dramatic demonstrations (enactments) of the prophetic words that he gave. God used him much more than any other prophet in terms of prophetic enactment. The prophetic enactments were so important to his ministry, that God allowed his wife to die and used Ezekiel's reaction to the death as a prophetic enactment (Ezekiel 24: 15-24). I believe that Ezekiel's foundation as a priest (being already conversant with the ways of God, which put a fear of God in his heart) helped him to be able to carryout every one of his dramatic assignments, which we will agree were very daring. Ezekiel's life as a priest, then prophet shows us that God knows what type of preparation is needed for anyone to go through before they begin to function in their destined calling. So do not cut short your training season if you want to be successful like Ezekiel.

The Prophet Haggai

This prophet is an example of one that certifies that the prophetic office is not just to call people to repent of sins of commission, but also that of omission. In other words, a prophet can correct a person where they may have missed the vision and purpose of God in their lives and ministry. The book of Haggai gives a practical situation where God can use a prophet to instruct a people, or person for the purpose of directing them to correct their wrong in performing a task.

Haggai was amongst the first people to return to Jerusalem from exile in Babylon after seventy long years. They returned in 538 BC and started building the temple in 536 BC. Haggai served as prophet around 520-518 BC, and he was the first to prophecy to the people after their return from captivity. The people had stopped building the temple and had become nonchalant. So God sent them a prophet. Haggai's assignment was to instruct or call God's people to complete the rebuilding of the temple.

> In the second year of Darius the king, in the sixth month, in the first day of the month, came the word of the LORD by Haggai the prophet unto Zerubbabel the son of Shealtiel, governor of Judah, and Joshua the son of Josedec, the high priest, saying, Thus speaketh the LORD of

host, saying, This people say, The time is not come, the time that the LORD's house should be built. Then came the word of the LORD by Haggai the prophet saying, is it time for you, O ye, to dwell in your cieled houses, and this house lie waste? Now therefore thus saith the LORD of host; consider your ways. Ye have sown much, and bring in little; ye eat, but ye have not enough; ye drink, but ye are not filled with drink; ye clothe you, but there is none warm; and he that earneth wages earneth wages to put it in a bag with holes. Thus saith the LORD of hosts; Consider your ways. Go up to the mountain, and bring wood, and build the house; and I will take pleasure in it, and I will be glorified, saith the LORD.

Haggai 1:1-8

The word of the LORD through Haggai was very clear: build God's house or there will be no prosperity in the land. Wow! Imagine a prophet of today giving a similar message from God to a minister of the gospel, telling him to make decisions that will benefit God's people and not only himself in ministry; telling him to build God's house or bring a curse on himself. The prophet will have to be bold to deliver such a message, because it is not an easy word to give. Also, it will take a matured minister, one who fears the LORD and has respect for the office of a prophet to receive this kind of message. That the message is "hard" however, should not stop any prophet from being obedient to his assignment. The prophet Haggai obeyed God and fulfilled his ministry.

The Prophet Zechariah

Zechariah who was a post-exilic prophet was a contemporary of Haggai. He served as prophet between 520-480 BC. He also encouraged the people to finish the rebuilding of the temple and in addition to this assignment, he prophesied to the people about the coming Messiah (Zechariah 2:10; 9:9). This prophet's ministry, just like that of Daniel, is an example of how God can and does speak to the prophet through very dramatic visions.

The book of Zechariah is filled with different kinds of visions (Zechariah 1:7-21, 2:1-2, 3:1-10, 4:1-14, 5:1-11, and 6:1-8), and each vision represented something different. Zechariah received most of his messages in visions, just like some people in the prophetic office do today. The question is, how does a prophet or anyone for that matter, handle visions and dreams especially if they are not understood? The way to handle it is to ask questions. Zechariah was first of all, quick to ask questions.

> I saw by night, and behold a man riding upon a red horse, and he stood among the myrtle tree that were in the bottom; and behind him were there red horses, speckled, and white. Then said I, O my LORD, what are these?
>
> Zechariah 1:8-9a

> Then lifted I up mine eyes, and saw, and behold four horns. And I said unto the angel that talked with me, what be these?
>
> Zechariah 1:18-19a

> I lifted up mine eyes again, and looked, and behold a man with a measuring line in his hand. Then said I, Whither goest thou?
>
> Zechariah 2:1-2a

Throughout this book the questions continue, and they are answered. It is imperative for a prophet to be quick in asking the meaning of the visions he or she receives. It does not matter whether an answer is gotten immediately, or later, the important factor is that interpretation is asked of the LORD and God answers at His own time.

A prophet who receives symbolic visions or dreams and does not ask God for the interpretation (if not received immediately) will make a mistake and deliver the wrong message, especially a prophet in training who is not yet used to how God speaks. Therefore, it behooves those in the prophetic office—young or old, mature or in training—to be conversant with prophetic symbols and meanings from examples of the ministry of the biblical prophets, as well as asking God for revelation for the ones that may not be explicit in the Bible.

The Prophet Malachi

The prophet Malachi was the last prophet God sent to His people after they came back from exile. He served as prophet around 430 BC. Malachi's assignment was to tell the people of their sin in forsaking to worship God and the neglect of rebuilding the temple. He was also to confront the priest with their sin of offering unacceptable sacrifices to God (Malachi 1:7-14); leading others into sin (Malachi 2:7-9); breaking God's laws (Malachi 2:11-16); and disrespecting God's name (Malachi 1:6). Furthermore, he was to make the people aware that they were calling evil good, and taking God's tithes and offerings (Malachi 2:17 and 3:8-9). In fact the priest and the people had become complacent and lacked the fear of God.

Malachi had a hard task to perform because the priest's involvement in disobeying God's commandments made it more difficult to reach the people, and get them to repent. That the priests were involved in this sin did not stop Malachi from performing his duties as prophet. And it should not stop any prophet either when God gives us a word of rebuke to deliver to mighty men and women in ministry. If the recipient of a prophetic word is a minister, or even a prophet or prophetess, it should never deter the message being given, as long as that word is from God. Wisdom of course should be applied at all times in speaking forth a prophetic word, but not to the detriment of the word being compromised or one's obedience to God. The maturity of a prophet is most needed in situations like this that involves rebuking or correcting a person who should know better.

NEW TESTAMENT PROPHETS

It is important to note that the ministry of the prophets in the Old Testament is slightly different from that in the New Testament. This difference is in relation to how God deals with us in the new covenant. In the old covenant, Jesus had not come, died, and resurrected, so the Holy Spirit was not residing in God's people. This means that they could not hear God for themselves and as such had to depend almost a hundred percent on the prophets to hear what God was communicating to His people.

In the dispensation of the new covenant, the Holy Spirit now resides in the believer allowing us to hear God for ourselves. Therefore, the believer does not have to depend on the prophet to hear God. However, the prophets are still needed because many believers though they have the Holy Spirit, still do not hear God when He speaks to them, choose to ignore God when He speaks to them, or need a confirmation after God have spoken to them. In such situations, God sends the believer a prophet.

The Prophet John

John was the first prophet mentioned in the New Testament. He was a miracle baby filled with the Holy Spirit from his mother's womb (Luke 1:5-15). John was a fulfillment of a prophecy given in Malachi (4:5). John had a great mantle with very specific assignments.

> And many of the children of Israel shall he turn to the LORD their God. And he shall go before him in the spirit and power of Elias, to turn the hearts of the fathers to the children, and the disobedient to the wisdom of the just; to make ready a people prepared for the LORD.
>
> Luke 1:16-17

Before John was born, he was called to be a prophet (like Jeremiah, and I believe all those in the five-fold ministry), and his ministerial blue print was given to his father, who was a priest not a prophet, so that he could allow and help John to become who God had called him to be. It is important to note that John was to be the next prophet or "brand new prophet" after there had been no prophetic ministry for a long time. The people had become a law unto themselves and sin was running rampant with no one to warn them of their evil ways. Then it was time for God to bring His people back to Himself, but this time in a closer relationship than the one in the past.

God have established it that when He wants to do something new he sends forth His prophets to prepare the people. So it was that it became the time for the LORD Jesus to come, which would bring the relationship of man closer to God. God sent John to prepare the way for the coming of His Son. This John did by confronting the people with their sins, thus bringing to their awareness the need for repentance. This awareness made the people desire to be forgiven, and it made them look for how to be forgiven; this prepared them for the ministry of Jesus. Hence John was a forerunner of Jesus. He went about preaching the baptism for the repentance of sin. God does send His prophets to prepare the people when something new is about to happen, or when there is a shifting of things in the spirit realm. Some people may not agree with this, but I believe it to be true and this is why God said in Amos 3:7, that He does not do anything without first revealing it to His servants, the prophets. I am not saying that God needs permission before He does anything, but that He allows His prophets to get a wind of it so that they can prepare the people by praying for them, by telling the people by prophetic utterances or by teachings and preaching.

John prepared the people by preaching. And I believe that in this dispensation that we are in, God has raised and is raising prophets to prepare

His people for the end time, His second coming. You might ask, "Isn't every preacher, prophet, or not preparing the people for the end times?" The answer is "yes," every minister has a part to play, however, the prophetic ministry is known to correct, rebuke, instruct, and call people back to repentance in a way that the other four fold offices do not. This is due to the gifts of this office. That is why you do not see most prophets preaching or teaching topics like prosperity, healings, and overcoming, to mention a few. Instead their messages are usually in the lines of repentance, righteousness, holiness, prayer, and the likes. It is not that the prophet does not believe, or sometimes speak on the other messages cited. It is that God uses them to speak more on issues and things that will stir or encourage the people to remain holy and sanctified before God. For this reason, God is releasing the prophets more so now and onward to prepare the people for His second coming, just like John came before Jesus first coming. So if you are a prophet, be prayerfully prepared for the great assignment ahead of you.

The Prophetess Anna

Anna the prophetess did not have a great mantle as that of Deborah but was just as powerful in her assignment. By great, I mean she did not lead a nation to war neither did she judge one. However, she was powerful because she was an intercessor. As we know, as Christians, nothing will be accomplished except there is prayer to back it up. The life style of Anna as an intercessor, is an example of what God requires of every one called to the prophetic office.

The Bible gives as an insight of how this woman lived her life.

> And there was one Anna, a prophetess, the daughter of Phanuel, of the tribe of Aser: she was of a great age, and had lived with an husband seven years from her virginity; And she was a widow of about fourscore and four years, which departed not from the temple, but served God with fastings and prayers night and day.
>
> Luke 2:36-37

This woman lived by fasting and praying all the time and never departed from the temple. This is why I say that she was powerful. In order to be successful as a prophet, we must live a life that is very prayerful and not depart from God's presence. This point cannot be overemphasized; for it is in staying in God's presence that we are sharp to hear what God is speaking to us (the prophet cannot afford to make mistakes because we can then make other people make mistakes). Anna did not depart from the temple; in her days the temple was made with hands. But now we are the temple of God, therefore, we cannot afford to pollute the temple so that God will not depart. It is imperative that every believer keeps his temple sanctified even more so the prophet. God will not continue to speak to a prophet who will not present his body holy and acceptable unto God.

The prophetess Anna knew and recognized the LORD Jesus Christ even as a babe.

> And she coming in that instant gave thanks likewise unto the LORD, and spake of Him to all them that looked for redemption in Jerusalem (Luke 2:38).

The question is how did she know that the baby was the LORD? She indeed was living a prayerful life, no doubt, because the Bible says so. Part of her assignment, I believe must have been intercession just for this purpose (for the Messiah to come), and this was why she recognized Him as a baby. And what joy she must have felt on the day of fulfillment. A day she came face to face with the king of the whole universe. What assignment for intercession has the LORD given to you as a prophet or prophetess? Are you being faithful to it and not slacking in any way? God is watching and requires obedience, especially in this area where nobody sees you, but Him. Let us remember to be like Anna and spend time in prayer without ceasing.

The Prophets Agabus, Silas, and Judas

These are typical examples of prophets in the New Testament found in the body of Christ today. Too many a time, I have heard preachers and non preachers, say that the prophetic, and the prophets ended with the

Old Testament. That after Jesus Christ came, died, and resurrected, we no longer need nor have prophets in the church. When John the Baptist is used as an example of a prophet in the New Testament, the answer to that by skeptics is that John's ministry was in operation at the same time as Jesus ministry on earth. They go further to say that the Holy Spirit was not yet poured out, or given to us at that time. They also teach that after the Holy Spirit came to reside in believers, and He now speaks to us, the office, hence the ministry of the prophet was abolished. They forget the truth that Ephesians chapter four talks about the five-fold amongst which the prophet is mentioned. Well, here in the book of Ephesians while the Holy Spirit is already indwelling in us are those called prophets by God (for every word in the Bible is given by inspiration by the God as written in 2 Timothy 3:16). When God called them prophets, it is because He knows that prophets are still needed in the church today, to perform that which He had set them in place for, from the beginning, otherwise, there would be no need to include them in the New Testament book.

There are some believers who agree that there are prophets in the body of Christ, but believe that the New Testament prophets are to only give words of encouragements (inspiration), and not words that instruct, direct, correct, or rebuke. In other words they are to only operate in the gift of prophecy and not word of knowledge, wisdom, or discerning of spirits. It is important to note that the Bible disagrees with this concept. The book of Acts 11:27-28 records that Agabus gave a prophetic word that there will be great dearth throughout the world, and that this word came to pass in the days of Claudius Caesar. The manifestation of this word proved that Agabus was a prophet of God. According to the word of God, when the word of a prophet comes to pass, then you know that he or she was sent by God. Therefore, if Agabus was a prophet, and he was in the New Testament and gave a non inspiring prophetic word, then prophets can and do declare words form God at times that are not to sooth our feelings. In fact this same Agabus was sent to the Apostle Paul when he was in Caesarea.

> And as we tarried there many days, there came down from Judaea a certain prophet, named Agabus. And when he was come unto us, he took Paul's girdle, and bound his own hands and feet, and said, Thus saith the Holy Ghost, So shall the Jews at Jerusalem bind the man that owneth this girdle, and shall deliver him into the hands of the Gentiles.
>
> Acts 21:10-11

It is obvious that this was not an encouraging word, because the people who heard it began to weep for Paul and told him not to go to Jerusalem. But Paul said that he was ready to go and be killed for the name of the LORD Jesus. What Paul never said was that Agabus was lying. True to the words of the LORD by Agabus, Paul was bound when he went to Jerusalem (Acts

22:24-25). As it was in the Old and the New Testament prophets, so it still is in this day. God uses His prophets to declare whatever kind of word that He chooses, encouraging, warnings, instructions, corrections, or rebuke. The purpose of the office has not, neither will it, change. In fact, the office of the prophets is needed more now in the church than ever before, to help keep the body of Christ in check.

Other examples of prophets whose names are mentioned in the New Testament are Silas and Judas (Acts 15:32). These men were sent by the apostles and elders with Paul and Barnabas, from Jerusalem to Antioch to read the letters written by them to the brethren. After reading the letters, Silas and Judas also exhorted the people with many words. (Acts 15:22-32). These prophets did not just read what they were given; they exhorted the people and confirmed (strengthened) them. That means that they encouraged them by the word of God (they preached), and I believe that they strengthened them by prophetic utterances. Prophets, therefore, are not just called to say, "Thus said the LORD," but also to preach and to teach as the LORD allows.

Apart from these prophets in the likes of those aforementioned, there are also other prophets in the Bible whose names were not mentioned, but were simply referred to as "a man of God" (1 Kings 13:1-3; 2 Chronicles 25:7-8) or "certain prophets" (Acts 13:1). Although these people's names were not written in the scriptures, their assignments were as crucial as every other prophet in the Bible.

WHO IS A PROPHET?

A prophet or prophetess is one whom God has called to the prophetic office. A believer cannot call him or her self to this office neither can another person do the calling. It is strictly like the other four fold, a gift of Jesus to the church. The prophetic ministry is not one that a believer evolves into. By this I mean it is not a graduation from one title to another. For example, a deacon after a while graduates to a prophet. No! The five-fold is a calling from the beginning. However, the person may function or even be ordained into other ministries before that of the prophetic office.

God sometimes allows a person to function in other parts of ministry to train and prepare them for their primary call, and at other times, the person functions, or is ordained directly into the office of their primary calling. That is, a prophet or pastor is ordained directly into their respective offices without being first ordained as a deacon or any other position in the church.

There are some instances where a person is called into more than one office. For example an individual can be a prophet as well as a pastor or a teacher as well as an evangelist. That means he may function simultaneously in these offices, or one at a given time or season. The most common way it has been is to function in one of the offices and then enter into the other and function in them simultaneously. It is simultaneous, because you do not loose the first office in which you functioned in when it is time for the second office to commence; although there may be periods of dormancy in one office, most of the time in the office in which you first functioned. It is God who ultimately determines the sequence of events that leads to one functioning in the prophetic, or any other office the same time or one at a time. Though God is the one that orchestrates everything, there is still a basic pattern to which these events occur. This pattern is foundational to the effective functioning of that person with the call, and it includes: knowing that you are called to an office, inner witnessing, other witnesses and confirmations, a period of training, and functioning in full in the office. Although the pattern is the same for all the five-fold ministries, there are however, events within this basic pattern that vary from one call to another, and from one individual to another as God allows. Since this book is about the prophetic office, the subsequent listing of events within the basic pattern is tailored as a guideline for those called to this office.

Knowing that You are Called

There is no set method or formula that explains or defines how to know that you are called to this ministry, it is different for many people and happens in diverse ways. However, there are some pointers or road maps that can help bring the person to this knowledge. There are several of such pointers of which a few are dealt with in this study.

Inner Witness

This is usually the first indication to most people to knowing that they are called to the prophetic office. The spirit of God in a person will bring to light that which He has called the person to do. In most cases, in order for the spirit of God to bring about this revelation, the person has been desiring and asking God about His purpose and plan for their lives, while at other times (less frequently) God reveals it without the person seeking to know. It is important to note that praying to God reveals His plan and purpose for our lives; this does not mean, that when we pray, we should ask, "am I a prophet or a pastor." Approaching the issue of our calling in this manner is not the proper way although it is not entirely wrong. The appropriate way is to keep declaring in prayer such words like "I will fulfill God's plan and purpose for my life." A person that is truthful about this will definitely become all that God wants him or her to be in life, and if functioning in one of the five-fold ministry is part of it then it will certainly come to pass. Also, being a servant in the house of God can help bring to our knowledge our calling. As we continue to be faithful to God's purpose in service, He begins to bring out of us those gifts, which He has deposited. We begin to notice that there are some aspects of ministry that we flow more easily in than others; and not just us, but others begin to notice them as well. For example, a person may notice that he or she knows things about people or events when they pray, but cannot really explain how. At other times, they may dream and more often than not, it comes to pass. What is happening here is that the spiritual senses are being sharpened? Now for such a person, it will not be abnormal at this point to ask God in prayer if he or she is called to be a prophet.

Let us consider another example. A person, who likes to pray all the time for other people's needs is called an intercessor. If this intercessor begins to see or know other people's problems and heart's desires by revelation (word of knowledge and wisdom) when praying, and God gives prophetic words to speak to these people he is praying for; it is very appropriate at this point that this person should ask God if he is called to be a prophet. It is important to note that I am not implying nor confirming that everyone who begins to pray by revelation are prophets or prophetesses, because these gifts can be operated independently as given by the Holy Sprit without being a prophet. However, continuous manifestation of these particular gifts is a good indication of the right time to seek God concerning your calling.

Apart from these examples, there are times when God shows or tells someone that he or she is a prophet directly, without having ever manifested the gift of prophecy or any of the revelational gifts. God can speak directly to the person through dreams, visions, or in his heart. In such cases, the person's ability to believe what God had shown them, determines how quickly they will begin to manifest the gifts. There always has to be an inner witness. It is needed to be successful in the prophetic office. You see if you do not believe or are not convinced of what God has told you or what He has called you to be, no one else will believe it either. If you as a prophet do not believe what God puts in your mouth to say, then the recipient has no business believing it. That is why the Bible says that every man should prophesy according to his proportion of faith (Rom. 12:6). It is imperative that a prophet does not doubt his calling or he will never be able to prophetically speak. When a person is in doubt, he or she should remain in a place of prayer until they believe, or come to know that being a prophet is not their calling. If God is calling the person, He will make a way to bring His purpose to pass if that person is willing to obey and fulfill God's plan.

The importance of having an inner witness cannot be over emphasized. God always gives room for an inner witness. In the cited examples two different groups of people are seen. The first group of people got their inner witness from the manifestation of the gifts, while the second group's inner witness was God's words to them in visions, or dreams of being called to the office. In both cases, the experience builds confidence in them, which would enable them to believe more easily that God may have called them to the prophetic office,

Other Witnesses and Confirmations

God also uses, in addition to inner witnessing, other witnesses and confirmations to bring a person to the knowledge that you are a prophet or prophetess. Other people begin to notice the prophetic auction or anointing on the person's life. God uses them to confirm your call by their admission to whatever God spoke to them through you being accurate and true. God also sends a prophetic word through His prophets or any of His ministers to confirm that inner witness that you are a prophet.

It is also important to note that a person who never had an inner witness before can also receive a prophetic word that he or she is called to the prophetic office. But in most instances where this situation occurs, the person is usually young in age, young in Christ, or not even yet in Christ. So they really have no knowledge of the Bible or have minimal understanding of the workings of the Holy Spirit. Therefore, they could not discern nor understand the prophetic gift in them even if they manifested it. A more mature believer, on the other hand, is less susceptible to being ignorant of what may be happening when the gifts begin to be more evident in them. Hence, they are less surprised when told that they are called to be a prophet.

Period of Training

Every prophet is supposed to go through a period of training. The length and type of training process differs from one person to another, and God orchestrates it. However, one goal is common to all those called to this office, during the training period: the opportunity to grow in the prophetic gifts. The training process, therefore, is to help the prophet or prophetess to know, understand, and mature in how the gift works. The prophet during the period is also supposed to grow in intercession and prophetic praying. I would like to emphasize that most of the time the circumstances of the training period are not very likeable or appealing. In fact, the training period is usually painful and can involve suffering in one form or another. By suffering, I mean it is very hard on the flesh and one requires great focus, strength, and faith to stay on course. Any person who would finish the training process will become successful in their assignment as prophets. Success becomes inevitable because the ability to stay and graduate from the training process builds character in the person that enables him or her to understand God and the call better. This helps the prophet to remain faithful to the office and obedient to God. Such a person does not need to worry about pride, arrogance, or self-gain because in the process of training, these things are purged out, and God will keep a prophet in the training stage until His will becomes God's own, before He will release the person to other people.

A prophet who is full of pride, arrogant, and makes a lot of mistakes is one who has not allowed himself to be fully processed in training; and is one who has released himself to others as a prophet. A fully processed prophet has less chance of errors in prophetic utterances in their ministry. The reason for this is that they become used to how to hear from the Holy Spirit during the training and also learn how to apply wisdom in delivering a word. Furthermore, they grow in boldness (not cockiness), which is always needed in the effective functioning of this ministry.

In addition to this form of training that is specifically done by the Holy Ghost, a prophet can also be trained by being mentored by an older prophet. Of course the older prophet is led of the Holy Spirit on how to mentor the trainee; it however, involves the trainee watching the older prophet as he or she functions in the office as well as the older prophet having teaching or seminar sections with the trainee. For example, the School of Prophets in the Old Testament headed by Elijah and Elisha at different times as well as Elijah mentoring Elisha one on one. This type of training, though not common, is still available in the church.

Release to Function in the Office

The release to fully function in the prophetic office comes after the prophet has successfully gone through the other stages. At this point, he really knows his calling and understands the gifts and responsibilities of the office; he has begun to manifest the gifts more accurately, and those around him now recognize him as a true prophet. He is being used by God to reach others who are not around him, for example, those who are neither in his local church nor close friends or family. The prophet may or not be anointed or ordained as a minister at this point, but that should not stop him from his obligations and duties as a prophet. Sometimes the local assembly (if they do not have a problem with the prophetic office) will either anoint or ordain the prophet to make it official, while at other times, the prophet never gets this acknowledgement for one reason or another. If this is the case, the person should continue to function in the office as he hears God. If needed for the successfully completion of the prophet's assignment, God would make sure that an official acknowledgement is achieved one way or another for the prophet. The prophet should not try to take a short cut and compromise who he is in the LORD by trying to make it happen by himself. It is God who calls anyone to this office. And when He calls, He anoints (separate), and ordains (acknowledgement), even before the prophet becomes aware of it. Thus, whatever is needed—procedure or protocol—God is able, and He will make it happen for the person.

The Gift of Prophecy Versus the Office of a Prophet

The gift of prophecy and the office of a prophet have been confused to be the same for too long by a lot of people in the church. It is believed by many that anyone who can prophesy is a prophet. This misunderstanding has indeed resulted from the lack of teaching in the body of Christ about the prophetic office as well as the gift of prophecy. The gift of prophecy is a gift of the Holy Spirit to the believer (any believer), while the office of a prophet is the gift of Jesus to some and not every believer in the church.

That the gift of prophecy is made available to the believer does not mean that everyone will manifest it either; however, it is made available to be desired (1 Corinthians 14:1) by all who becomes born again. It is the most emphasized gift that a believer should want to manifest (1 Corinthians 14:22, 39), but then the Holy Spirit still appropriates it as He wants (wills). In contrast the office of a prophet is not entered into, because it was desired by anyone; it is instead a calling into one of the extensions of Jesus ministry when He was on earth.

At His ascension, He gave this five-fold ministry, of which the prophetic is one of them to the church as a gift for effective running of the church. Ephesians 4:11 clearly states that all are not called into this five-fold ministry, thus all are not called to be prophets. It can be argued that 1 Corinthians 12 says the same about spiritual gifts not being for everybody (to one is given the gift of miracles, to another prophecy), therefore, those that do have the gift of prophecy have to be prophets. This argument, however, is settled by 1 Corinthians 14:31 and 39, which says we are to covet earnestly the best gifts and then covet prophecy; which suggest that prophecy is the best gift and should be desired by all believers. It is necessary to emphasize that these verses did not say covet to be prophets, instead Paul poses a question in verse 29 are all prophets.

Paul in 1 Corinthians 12 addressed both the gift of the spirit as well as the gift of Jesus. He talks about the different gifts of the spirit in verses 1-11 and 12-29 talks about there being many members in one body. Paul teaches that there are many parts that are called to work in the church, and he uses the illustration of the different parts of the body to explain different roles that the body parts play, and then he likened this to the body of Christ. His point being that everyone in the church cannot function in the same role, or there will be functions that will not be performed. For this reason, Paul says that God hath set in the church, apostles, prophets, and other gifts, before he asked the questions if all are apostles or prophets. In other words, all are not apostles or prophets; neither are all teachers, evangelist, or pastors. It is, therefore, not everyone who has the gift of prophecy that is a prophet, but every prophet must have this gift.

There is a story in the Bible that talks about the daughters of Phillip. Acts 21:8-9 says that these four women do prophesy. What I find interesting is that the next verse talks about a prophet Agabus. So the question is, why did Paul not refer to Phillip's daughters as prophetesses? Instead of just saying that they prophesy, and then immediately writes about Agabus the prophet and not that he prophesies. The reason is that there is a difference between the office and the gift. In the church today, there are many people who manifest this gift and so think or believe that they are called to the prophetic office when they are not. What great confusion. No wonder some of those who are really called to the office do not understand if they are called. There has been a lacking in teaching and training for the prophetic office in the church for too long, hence the confusion. It is my prayer that this book will help to reduce if not eradicate this confusion in the lives of all who reads it in Jesus name. Amen.

Are You a Prophet?

1. Do you think that you are called to the prophetic office?

2. Why do you think you are called to the prophetic office?

3. Which of the gifts of the prophetic office do you manifest? (it should be obvious to those in your local church)

4. Do you like to intercede a lot?

5. Do people come to you often to pray for their needs and you receive insight on how to prophetically pray?

6. Do you have dreams and visions that more often than not come to pass?

7. Do you love to worship and pray?

8. Do you easily sense things about people and places and later realize that what you sensed did happen?

9. Have you ever received a prophetic word that you are called to be a prophet, or are a prophet?

10. What is your favorite group in church?

These questions only serve as a guide to help you determine if you are called to the prophetic office or not. If you truthfully answered "yes" to questions 1 and 4-9, answered the word of wisdom, word of knowledge, and prophecy to question 3, and your favorite group is the prayer group, then answer question 2 with a written essay and submit it to your council of elders in your church and pray that they are led by God on what to do with your essay. I pray that if you are a prophet or prophetess, God's will for your life in this calling will not be aborted. In Jesus name, Amen.

TYPES OF PROPHETS

There are different types of prophets within the prophetic office. Based on their assignments, there are apostolic prophets, evangelical prophets, teaching prophets and pastoral prophets. All of these types of prophets have an additional calling into one or more of the other four-fold ministry. That some prophets have more than one calling does not make one better, superior or more anointed than the other. It just means that the scope of their work is different and tailored to what God has called each one to perform. These prophets can function in the other offices simultaneously with that of the prophetic, or when the other calling becomes manifest at a later part in their prophetic office or vice versa. They however do not stop being prophets because they are also apostles, teachers, pastors, or evangelist. Some prophets may not be called to any other of the remaining four fold, they may have the anointing to write prophetic books or prophetic songs. However, majority of the prophets seen today are simply prophets. All they do is to declare the word of God. They do not pioneer any work, teach, operate any power gift nor write books or songs.

In addition to this subgroup of prophets there are also false and immature prophets in the body of Christ. It is important that the church is able to discern or recognize the different types of prophets. For better understanding, let us look at some examples.

Apostolic Prophets

Moses had an assignment that was apostolic. The apostle taking from the Greek word *apostolos* means "the sent one." They are sent to break ground, to pioneer a work, to bring a revelation of the word of God like never known before by the help of the Holy Spirit. The apostolic office usually has signs and miracles following it. The twelve apostles were sent to different parts of the world to spread the good news of Jesus Christ. The Apostle Paul was sent to the Gentiles and the Jews with a revelation of Jesus that even the first apostles were not privy to. A work (revelation) was committed to him that revolutionized the Jews thinking about salvation and justification, especially as it applied to the Gentile nation. This was new to the Jews. Moses was sent to deliver the Israelites and bring them to the promise land, a task that was never done before. In addition, he was to lead them through wars and guide them through the wilderness for forty years. Indeed Moses broke ground and pioneered a work. A revelation of God as "I am" was committed to him to bring to the people, as well as other revelations about God's nature. The Ten Commandments was also given to Moses. This prophet did a lot of things that were never done or seen before, and signs and miracles were not strange to his ministry. He easily functioned if it were to be in this day in the office of the five-fold ministry, a true exhibit of the apostolic calling. Moses was a true apostle, even if the word was not used then in the Old Testament, but God called him a prophet. Why? Because Moses's first calling was to be a prophet. Also, at that time, the LORD Jesus had not yet come; hence the revelation of the apostolic ministry was not yet known. Moses the apostolic prophet was also anointed to write. He wrote the first five books of the Bible: Genesis, Exodus, Leviticus, Numbers, and Deuteronomy.

Another example of an apostolic prophet is Abraham. He was called a prophet in Genesis 20:7. Abraham was not the typical "thus saith the LORD" prophet, either. He did not give any prophecies nor perform any miracles, neither was his walk with God as dramatic as that of Moses. However, he was a great prophet, one who walked with God in obedience and reverence. But his assignment was apostolic. He was sent by God to leave his own kindred and people and go to a place he did not know because God desired a people whom He would call His own. Before Abraham, nothing like that had ever happened. Abraham pioneered a work, he allowed himself to become God's poster for obedience. He started the faith movement, which is still being talked about and studied today. He got the revelation of what faith is and means; for there is no other way that Abraham could have believed God by himself (considering all he had to go through with no reference point on faith). God gave him the ability to believe Him, so we can say that the revelation of faith was committed to Abraham, and that is why he is called the Father of Faith.

Moses and Abraham as prophets had very similar assignments. They were sent to a specific place and had a revelation of God that was not known before, which changed the people's way of doing things. Just like Moses and Abraham, there are prophets in our dispensation that have an apostolic work. Their assignments are pioneering when categorized, and the content of the messages spreads through out the body of Christ, to affect our way of thinking and cause a change in the lives of those who embrace it.

The Evangelical Prophets

The work of the evangelist in the body of Christ is primarily to preach salvation and help to bring souls to the kingdom of God. They go out to preach, and people give their lives by the conviction of the Holy Spirit to Christ. An example of an evangelist in scripture is Philip (Acts 21:8). The power gifts (healings, faith, and miracles) are supposed to be associated with this ministry (I am not saying that they cannot be operated by one who is not an evangelist). Sometimes the evangelist operates in these powerful gifts, which helps to bring the people to have faith much quicker and receive Christ. In like manner, an evangelical prophet operates in the power gifts. Examples of such prophets are Elijah and Elisha, although during the time of these prophets, Jesus had not yet come; hence the words *gospel* and *evangelical* did not exist. However, the miracles and wonders that these prophets did—if it were in the New Testament—will fall under the category of power gift.

It is obvious that one of the reasons that Elijah and Elisha were such powerful prophets—who were respected and reckoned with—is because of the miracles, signs, and wonders that God did through them. Whenever these prophets brought a word from God, the people listened. A prophet or prophetess in this day that would manifest the power gifts in such magnitude, in addition to the vocal gifts already operating through them, would definitely be heard when he or she preaches repentance. The reason being that the people would see the awesome power of God, and their hearts would be opened to hear the word, and, in a matter of time, many souls would be led to the kingdom of God. Evangelical prophets are not very common in the church today.

Teaching and Pastoral Prophets

A prophet who is also a teacher of the Word falls into this subgroup. It is imperative to know that I am not referring to preaching, but teaching, because there is a difference. Almost every believer can preach, but the percentage of teachers is few. A teacher can expound the word of God given by the Holy Spirit with simplicity. Most teaching prophets are stewards of ministries and/or ministry heads. Those called to be teachers prophetically teach the word of God. What this means is that God tells or shows them something that the people need to know or do in order to achieve or avert something; it then becomes the prophet's responsibility to make the people aware and understand what God is saying through biblical teachings. Some teaching prophets have schools to train others called into the prophetic office. Some biblical examples are Elijah, Elisha, and Samuel.

Samuel and Deborah were both judges in Israel. In order to lead and judge the people, they must know and understand the word of God and communicate it to the people. In view of this, I suggest that Samuel and Deborah were teaching prophets. Some teaching prophets also have the anointing to write what God wants the people to know in books. It is my belief that prophets Isaiah, Jeremiah, Ezekiel, and all the other prophets who wrote books, may have been teaching prophets, because the books written by them are being used as teaching materials in the church today.

Pastoral prophets are prophets that are also called to pastor a flock. That is they are resident pastors in churches or are the founding stewards of churches. In my opinion, pastoral prophets have the most difficult of all the combination callings. My reason is that one called to this particular dual office needs a lot of patience, wisdom, and maturity to be successful. They also have to be extra careful not to be obedient to man instead of God. The reason for this is when the prophetic nature is required of the pastor, for example to give a word of knowledge to a congregant about being in adultery, the pastor if not a man set out to please God alone, will not give the word to the person. This lack of obedience results from the fact that the pastor is worried about loosing his congregant. The pastor, not wanting this to be the case, will start to dance to the tune of the people instead of God, and such a person cannot be successful in ministry.

False Prophets

The word *false* is the most common word attached to prophets of today. There are many men and woman of God who are called false prophets when they are not. The church and the world have, in my opinion, totally misunderstood the meaning of the word as it relates to the prophetic office, as well as misused the word *false* in order to benefit themselves. Does that mean that there are no false prophets in the church today? Of course there are. But the sad thing is that the true, erring, and false prophets have been lumped into one because of lack of understanding.

When the Bible refers to false prophets, these where people who did not hear from God at all, but lied that they did, as well as people who deliberately set out to misguide another or turn him or her away from the truth. It does not in anyway refer to those prophets who have heard from God but delivered the message in a wrong way; these prophets lacked maturity. It also does not refer to those who were really convinced that they heard from God. These, not being trained in knowing the difference between hearing "themselves" and hearing from God, delivered the word thinking it was from God. In other words, they did not deliberately set out to deceive anyone. They lacked training.

It is also important to mention that true prophets have given God-given words for individuals, and yet they were called false prophets because the person did not like the word, or it took a while to manifest. (See the chapter on personal prophecies). Who then is a false prophet? The best way to explain this is by illustrations. Let us consider some examples of false prophets that are mentioned in scriptures.

The book of Jeremiah chapter 14 tells a story of how the children of Israel refused to repent of their evil ways, and God pronounced doom on them. The Bible records that the Prophet Jeremiah wanted to intercede on their behalf, for God not to destroy them, but God told him not to pray: That Israel would see the sword and famine, and that peace would elude them. Then Jeremiah said to God that there were some prophets who told Israel otherwise. This was God's response:

Then the LORD said unto me, The prophets prophesy lies in my name: I sent them not, neither have I commanded them, neither spake unto them: they prophesy unto you a false vision and divination, and a thing of nought, and the deceit of their heart.

Jeremiah 14:14

Let us examine what God said in this verse and bring out some key points.

1. Lies.

2. They were not sent.

3. They were not commanded.

4. They did not hear from God.

5. The vision was false.

6. It was divination.

7. It was nothing, meaning it will not come to pass because it was not from God.

8. They planned to deceive the people.

These are the factors that define a false prophet. If any one of these is named in the life of a "so called" prophet or prophetess, then they are false.

It is important to mention that for a person to be called false, because of one of these factors, it must be obvious to the church and not just to an individual or some people. The reason being that one person can have a grudge against the prophet, due to one situation or another. Another reason is if a word given took a longer time than anticipated, or did not come to pass for some personal reason (factors that affect personal prophecy), then the prophet is labeled false. For this reasons, one or all of these pointers should be obvious to a lot of people, preferably the church. The church (body of Christ) has to know by discernment, as well as experience, over time in looking at the ministry and the lifestyle of the "so called" prophet to be able to determine if he/she is true or false. That means then that only a true God-fearing, Holy Ghost-filled church or persons can know a false prophet. A false prophet, therefore, has to exhibit one or more of these points listed above. Let's examine some of these points in detail.

Point one says that the words spoken are lies, and eight says to deceive the people. The Bible tells us that the devil is the father of lies. In other words, when these false prophets speak, it is the devil that speaks through them. As we know, the devil comes to kill, to steal, and to destroy; therefore, the motive behind these words is to kill, to steal, or to destroy the person receiving it. It is to turn the person away from God's plan, which at that particular time may even include judgment. A false prophet can give words that are soothing to the ears, but it is not from God. It becomes easier for the word of the false prophet to be perceived as correct because it pleases the flesh, whereas the ulterior motive is to turn the person receiving the word away from God's plan. This was the case in the time of Jeremiah the prophet. False prophets arose to prophesy lies in the name of the LORD. The Bible says that they did this, for they thought that they could cause the people to forget the name of God (Jeremiah 23:26-27). The plan was deceit (If a person forgets the name of God, he/she has set themselves up for destruction). A false prophet tries to work against God's plan. But thank God for Jeremiah, a true prophet, whom God used to set the people straight.

Another example of a false prophet is in the book of Acts 13:4-12. In this story, the Apostle Paul, Barnabas, and John were in Salamis, where they preached the gospel of Jesus Christ in the synagogues of the Jews. Then they went to Paphos, where they found a Jew who was a false prophet named Bar-Jesus. The deputy of that country, Sergius Paulus, had requested Paul and his entourage to come and speak to him about the gospel. This false prophet tried to deceive the deputy from believing in Jesus. Paul, being full of the Holy Ghost, rebuked the false prophet and cursed him to be blind. In this story, we see that the false prophet again tried to go against God's plan, will, and purpose for the man. Now, let us look at some of the other pointers for recognizing a false prophet.

Point two and three says that the prophets were not sent nor commanded. The word *sent* means "to go" and *commanded* means "deputizing under another's authority" (in this case, God's authority). Therefore, these prophets were not asked to go anywhere with any message, neither did they have God's authority to speak as prophets. Therefore, any message delivered by such a person is definitely false. These kinds of false prophets deliberately make up stories, or the devil gives them one to tell. They may not have a motive to destroy or kill anyone; they may just want to be noticed, and/or heard in order to feel important, or they are wannabe prophets.

Point six talks about divination. This is an important point to take note of. The spirit of divination can be mistaken for the spirit of God if there is no gift of discerning of spirits in operation. It is a dangerous spirit that can and has crept into the church with a disguise of the prophetic. The dangerous thing about divination is that—unlike lies, which can be easily exposed—a diviner can actually speak words that are true, and as such, they are easily believable. A good example is observed in the book of Acts 16:16-18 where the Apostle Paul and his team were in Macedonia, and a woman who had the spirit of divination followed them for some days, saying, "These men are the servants of the Most High God, which shew unto us the way of salvation" (v. 17b).

On examining this word spoken by the woman, it cannot be disputed to be the truth, yet Paul rebuked her. The question is, why was she rebuked? Paul had to rebuke her because she was not speaking by the spirit of God, although she was correct. You see if Paul had not rebuked her for all to see and then delivered her from that demonic possession, the devil would have used the woman to deceive the people much more after Paul departed from that place. The devil's agenda for the believers in that city would have been propagated through the woman, for now, the people would think that it was God speaking to them prophetically, whenever the woman speaks—when really it was the devil. So it was imperative that Paul expose the spirit behind the woman's supposed gifts, even if she spoke the truth. In like manner today, there is the spirit of divination in the body of Christ that can speak as it were the true condition of what a person is going through in their lives, or what may have happened in the past. Thus, it is perceived as a word from God, when it is not.

This type of false prophet is the most dangerous kind and can very easily lead a believer astray if one is not careful, filled with the Holy Spirit, and knows the written word of God. The most accurate way to recognize such a false prophet is by the gift of discernment (which is what Paul used in this story), and also a study of the lifestyle of that prophet to see if it reflects the principles of God. You see, a false prophet cannot truly live according to the scriptures, nor can he exhibit the fruit of the spirit for that will be contrary to who he is, as well as his or her purpose.

Immature Prophets

In the body of Christ today, a lot of the prophets that are termed false are not; instead they made mistakes (err), hence the name immature prophets. What exactly does an immature prophet mean or do? As the name indicates, these prophets miss it one way or another. They make mistakes either by being pressured to prophesy when God is not speaking, or they are afraid to say the truth when He speaks. Also, they

are not mature enough to understand how the prophetic operates, or they are unable to apply wisdom
in their assignments. These prophets are called of the
LORD, they hear from God, but sometimes they dance
to the tune of the people instead of God. An example
is Prophetess Noadiah, who amongst other prophets,
tried to stop Nehemiah and the people from rebuilding the wall of Jerusalem when the people returned
from exile (Nehemiah 6:10-14). These prophets were
dancing to the tune of Tobiah and Sanballat who did
not want the wall rebuilt.

It is important for us to study some other examples
of an immature prophet so that we can understand it
better. Let us consider a situation, where God speaks
a word to a prophet to go and tell his boss at work to
stop stealing from the company funds. You will agree
with me when I say that this is a very difficult word
for any prophet to speak. The reason being that the
prophet has a lot at stake; he does not want to lose
his job. If the prophet is not matured, he will not give
the word at all, or he will deliver it in his own words
(not really the truth) in a way that will not cause him
his job. His motivation to go this route is fear. If the
prophet acts in fear, he will be in error. An example for
such scenario in the Bible is Samuel. In 1 Samuel 3:11-
14, God gave him a word for Eli the priest. The word
was that Eli's house will be judged for their iniquity,
and there will be no sacrifice or offering that will be
able to purge them.

In other words, Samuel was to tell his boss and mentor that he and his household have sinned against the LORD, that their sin will never be forgiven, and that destruction was inevitable. How do you deliver such a message to the man who practically raised you and taught you all that you know? It was definitely a difficult task; for the Bible records that he was afraid to tell Eli the vision (1 Samuel 3:15). However, he eventually spoke the words as the LORD told him. Samuel was not going to err in his first assignment as a prophet. A similar scenario is also seen in the case of the prophet Nathan. God sent him to King David to confront him of his sin. Now this sin was not "repent from idolatry or face the consequences" which was a more common word for the prophets in those days. This sin was one done in secret by the king who should have been an example to his subjects. And the worst thing was that he tried to cover this sin with another more grievous one. King David took another man's wife, got her pregnant, and then had the man killed (2 Samuel 11 and 12). This was the sin that Nathan was to confront David with and then proclaim that the child would die. I do not envy Nathan at all. How are you supposed to tell your king that what he thought he did in secret is really not a secret? How are you as a prophet supposed to go and tell your pastor that the sin he did in his bedroom has been made known to you by God, and that punishment was inevitable no matter how much he repented of that sin?

As prophets, we are sometimes faced with such dilemma. It may not be your boss at work or your pastor that you have to speak to; it may be someone else who you hold in high esteem, and you know he or she ought to know better than what they have done. What does the prophet do with such a task? He ponders on this assignment whether it should be done or not. So many reasons come to mind why we should not say anything. The most important one being "what if we are wrong," and the next closely following is "what if the person denies it even when it is true and then calls me false, what would I do?" These questions and more disturb the mind of the prophet, though he or she knows that they heard God very well. We allow how other people might perceive us control and rule our decision, instead of being ruled by God only. At this point erring is very possible. Because when we do give the word, we try to say it in a way that will please the person and most times lose the exact message to be delivered; or we water it down and the effect is not the same on the recipient. In the circumstance with King David, the Prophet Nathan did not mince words, though he gave the message as a parable as God led him. When David said the punishment that such a person who could do such a thing deserves, Nathan said to David "Thou art the man." If Nathan had not gone about delivering the word, as I believe he was directed, King David probably would not have received the word the way that he did, and Nathan would have erred in his assignment. The king could have denied all of the allegations, and the people could have thought that Nathan was wrong.

Let us look at a hypothetical example where a prophet can make a mistake. God sends a prophetess to a church to fellowship with the people, at a service, the prophetic auction was great, and she was stirred to work in the gifts of the office. She heard a word for someone, and it was just that one word—*go*. Now the prophetess feels that one word is too little to say, so she adds the words *to school*. This now makes the word to become "go to school," here the prophetess has erred. In this case, pride is the likely cause of the error. Pride, because the prophetess felt that giving a monosyllable word does not make her look like a "big prophet," she decided to add words that God had not said. God, have mercy on us! If one is not careful, ego will and does cause errors in the ministry of prophets.

The other factor that was aforementioned that also result in prophets making mistakes is pressure. Everyone that operates in this office knows that there are times when the people or circumstances can put pressure on those in the prophetic office to give a word from God. For example, let us take a situation occurring in the prophet's home church family or within his natural family that warrants a prophetic word from God. The prophet, if not careful, will feel pressured to bring that word, especially if the people are asking him what God is saying. There is nothing wrong in the prophet being in expectation to hear from God and giving the word when God speaks. But if God does not speak and the pressure is still on, the prophet—in order to please the people, or prove that he still hears from God—can hear his own spirit and think it is God, thereby erring when he says what he heard. It is important that those called to this office do not allow anything or anyone to pressure them to speak when God is not speaking, thereby being led into error. This in itself could make a true prophet look false. This type of error in prophetic judgment will make people question the anointing and calling on that person's life. It is a pitfall that must be avoided at all cost.

Parking Lot Prophets

Parking lot prophets: I wonder whoever came up with such a name. It baffles me every time I think about or hear it. I can only come to one conclusion: the devil found a way to discredit and make mockery of the office of a prophet, and the church bought it all. It is sad to know that the people who use this description, most of them are ministers of the gospel, even those called to the prophetic office. My question to the people who use this term is, who or what is a "parking lot prophet"? It certainly is not scriptural, so where did it come from? Please do not misunderstand me. I know that the name refers to a person who speaks a prophetic word to somebody in the parking lot. But the question again is, what makes that wrong or a sin? Was the word spoken proven to be a lie? Is this person only known to give a prophetic word in the parking lot? Because if the answer to these last two questions are not yes, then what exactly is the problem? What is the scriptural backing for labeling a person who spoke a true word from God in the parking lot—a "parking lot prophet"?

Just because the word was uttered in the parking lot does not make it false. Until a person is proved to be a false prophet according to biblical definitions or principles, the church body has to be very careful about their pronouncements, before the people err themselves in pointing accusing fingers, especially if that finger is pointed at those whom God has called to occupy an office. Furthermore, the prophetic office seems to be the most targeted by the enemy (devil) because the main message of those called to it is one of holiness, righteousness, and repentance. Let us, as a church, not shoot each other in the foot anymore by helping the devil to succeed in his propaganda against truly living the abundant life that we have in Jesus the Christ.

CONCLUSION

The prophetic office and the ministry of a prophet should not be one that is mysterious or misunderstood. The prophets and prophetess are called to the body of Christ to perform a duty—a duty that is needed especially in this end times. Why this end time? Because God is coming for a church that has no spot or blemish. That is a church that will make the rapture. However, it is evident that the church at this point is not ready for the Master's return. What! With the lack of love for one another, backbiting, finger pointing, love of money more than the love for God, and all the other little things that the church is today, it is obvious that turning back to our first love (God) is desperately needed in other for the church to be where God wants it to be.

The people of God have left their first love and sought after other gods, just like in the time of old, the god of money, power, position, title, etcetera. Of course as Christians it is not wrong, nor is it a sin to have any of these things mentioned. But when these things take preeminence over the things of God in our lives, then we have missed the most important aspect of why we were created and have lost focus on the real (eternal) things.

Unfortunately, the body of Christ today is slowly losing focus on the things that matter the most. If this is not true, then why does the church have so much divorce, brethren killing one another, teenage pregnancies, ministers having extramarital affairs, pride, and arrogance in the pulpit, just to mention a few. It is obvious that the body of Christ needs an overhauling by the Holy Spirit in order for us to get it right again.

God is a God of dispensations and seasons. The five-fold ministry was set in place to help equip the body of Christ to stay on tract with the timetable of God. The pastors, evangelists, and teachers have been in the forefront of the five-fold for a while and have done and are still doing their work in the body. Then the ministry of the apostles began to be evident in the church to perform that which God had committed to them. But now, in this end time dispensation, the office of the prophet has been catapulted to the forefront. It is important to know that because the prophetic office is being brought to the forefront, it does not negate the operation of the other ministries. Rather the prophetic office is to help the other ministries function more effectively. Whether we believe it or not, accept it or not, the five-fold will be in effective operation till Jesus returns. Because Jesus Himself gave the ministry gifts to the church to enable her to come to the unity of faith and of the knowledge of the Son of God, unto a perfect man and unto the measure of the statute of the fullness of Christ. And all must fulfill this assignment in the body of Christ for there to be a church that can rapture. Hence, God is now sending His prophets (all of the sub-types) to His people to sound the alarm and to give the warning that the end is near, and we need to get our acts together and begin to please God.

The prophet is sent primarily to the church. Why is that? The reason is that God uses them to bring His message to reform the people. In the Old Testament, a prophet is usually seen when the king and the subjects have strayed from God's will and purposes, or when direction is needed. It is easy for the church to say that in this age we do not need a prophet to bring direction from God because the individual hears God for himself. That may be so. But in the case where the individual thought he heard from God and decided to go his own way anyway and then leads others astray, God will send that person a prophet to correct the errors of his/her ways. It is a known fact that the body of Christ—of course not everybody in the church but most people—has deviated from the truth of God's Word, despite numerous teachings, preaching, miracles, and signs. Instead we run after the miracles and signs instead of the giver of the miracles. Some ministers (prophets included) preach manipulative messages, instead of Holy Ghost–inspired ones. Indeed the church is not what it ought to be, and God is demanding perfection from us—perfection that comes from being a child of God. Sometimes, we think that to be perfect means we do not make any mistakes. Not really. Perfection means a mind and heart that is set to act according to the word of God at all times, and when one falls short of this, repentance is immediate.

God is calling the church to perfection and is sending the prophets to help bring this message—the message of holiness and righteousness without which no man shall see God. Why is God specifically sending the prophets? Because this is the primary assignment of the prophetic office and since we are in the end times, God has released them from the nooks and corners, from their hiding places to perform their duty in declaring the word of God. This word is to be declared, however, He instructs, in order to help prepare the body of Christ, for the second coming of our LORD and Savior, Jesus, the Christ. With this in mind, the next time you see or hear a prophet of God, instead of your first reaction being one of criticism or persecution, stop for a moment to think about this book. Have an open mind. Perhaps God has a word for you personally, for the body of Christ in particular, or for the world in general. Make sure that before you reject the word as false, line it up with biblical principles to see if it passes the test, then pray for God to show you if the word is true or not. If you really address it in this manner, God will not allow you to receive a word that He has not sent.

The prophetic office is real and true, and the prophets have been released by God to perform a task in this end time. That Jesus is coming back soon is a fact that cannot be denied. The question is, are you prepared and ready for Him? This question should be what is uppermost in our minds. It is time to let all distractions in the body of Christ go, and we run the race to the end. It is time to work and walk together as a church, especially the five-fold ministry officers, to prepare the people with the help of the Holy Ghost, a body ready for the bridegroom. God bless you for reading this book. In Jesus name, Amen.